THE ROUGH GUIDE TO
Reading Music

and Basic Theory

A clear guide for anyone who
wants to learn how to read and write music,
and a handy reference book for anyone
who already can.

Hugo Pinksterboer

THE ESSENTIAL TIPBOOK

Publishing Details

This first edition published May 2001 by Rough Guides Ltd,
62–70 Shorts Gardens, London WC2H 9AH

Distributed by the Penguin Group:
Penguin Books Ltd, 27 Wrights Lane, London W8 5TZ
Penguin Putnam, Inc., 375 Hudson Street, New York, NY 10014
Penguin Books Australia Ltd, 487 Maroondah Highway, PO Box
257, Ringwood, Victoria 3134, Australia
Penguin Books Canada Ltd, 10 Alcorn Avenue, Toronto, Ontario,
Canada M4V 1E4
Penguin Books (NZ) Ltd, 182–190 Wairau Road, Auckland 10,
New Zealand

Typeset in Glasgow and Minion to an original design by
The Tipbook Company bv

Printed in The Netherlands by Hentenaar Boek bv, Nieuwegein

160 pp

A catalogue record for this book is available from the British
Library.
1-85828-846-0

THE ROUGH GUIDE TO
Reading Music
and Basic Theory

Written by

Hugo Pinksterboer

ROUGH
GUIDES

THE ESSENTIAL TIPBOOK

Rough Guide Tipbook Credits

Journalist, writer and musician **Hugo Pinksterboer** has written hundreds of articles and reviews for international music magazines. He is the author of the reference work for cymbals (*The Cymbal Book*, Hal Leonard, US) and has written and developed a wide variety of musical manuals and courses.

Illustrator, designer and musician **Gijs Bierenbroodspot** has worked as an art director in magazines and advertising. While searching in vain for information about saxophone mouthpieces he came up with the idea for this series of books on music and musical instruments. Since then, he has created the layout and the illustrations for all of the books.

Acknowledgements

Concept, design and illustrations: Gijs Bierenbroodspot

Translation: The Tipbook Company bv

Contributing editor: Duncan Clark

IN BRIEF

This Rough Guide is a concise, easily digestible introduction to reading and writing music, and it explains the basic principles of music theory, from scales and keys to transposition and the circle of fifths. It's also a handy reference tool for players who can already read music, including clear definitions of hundreds of foreign and technical terms.

Valuable skills
When you've read and understood this book, you'll be equipped not only to read music, but also to understand more about what you're playing. You'll also be in a better position to transcribe music from CDs, for example, and to write and arrange your own music.

Whatever you play
This book is aimed at all musicians – from heavy-metal guitarists to classical flautists. It's written in a user-friendly style, and is full of easy-to-play examples and practical tips.

Use a keyboard
You'll find it useful to have some kind of keyboard at hand as you go through this book. You don't need to know how to play it, and any basic model will do.

Glossary
The glossary at the end of the book provides quick answers to many questions, and also acts as an index.

CONTENTS

1. READING MUSIC

This chapter outlines some of the advantages of being able to read and write music, and explains how to get the most out of this book.

In all genres except classical music, there are many famous players who can't read a note of music. And millions of songs have been composed by musicians who've never put anything down on paper. But if you *do* read music…

- You have access to **loads of sheet music**, including songs and pieces by your favorite band or composer, as well as study material.
- You can **play along** with groups who use sheet music right away.
- You can also **write music** – tunes and exercises, for example, or a part for a bass player or brass section, or an idea for a solo. Writing something down is easier than remembering it – especially in the long run.
- **Talking to other musicians** is a lot easier. You'll never be dumbstruck by talk of a B flat major scale, a fifth, or an eighth note.
- **It's easier to understand** the structure of music – from single chords to whole pieces – and how and why it works the way it does.

By heart
Being able to read music doesn't mean you always have to play from paper. Classical musicians usually do, but music stands are rare on rock, blues and jazz stages. Sheet music allows you to play things that others have written, but once you know a piece by heart, it may very well sound better if

1

you play it without the music – you'll be able to concentrate on how the notes are supposed to sound, rather than on which ones you're supposed to play.

WHAT TO FIND WHERE

The first ten chapters of this Rough Guide introduce everything you need to know to actually read a piece of music. Chapters 2–5 look at the basics of rhythm (when to play the notes and how long they should last) and pitch (how high or low the notes should be). Chapters 6–9 deal with *how* the notes should be played: loud or soft, fast or slow, aggressively or lyrically, and with or without ornaments. Chapter 10 deals with repeat signs and section markings.

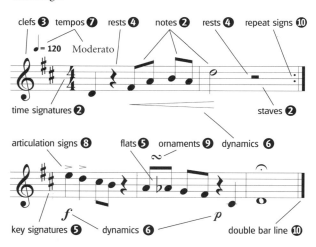

How long notes should last: **CHAPTER 2**	How loud to play: **CHAPTER 6**
Beats and measures: **CHAPTER 2**	How fast to play: **CHAPTER 7**
The stave and clefs: **CHAPTER 3**	How to 'pronounce' the notes: **CHAPTER 8**
High and low notes: **CHAPTER 3**	Musical ornaments: **CHAPTER 9**
Sharps and flats: **CHAPTER 5**	Repeat and section signs: **CHAPTER 10**

Chapters 11–15

Chapters 11–15 look at some basic theory. You don't neces-sarily need all this information to read music 'note by note', but without a basic knowledge of scales and intervals you'll never be able to read fluently, or really understand what you're playing or writing.

Chapters 16–20

Chapters 16–19 cover some more useful areas: transposi-tion, metric accents, irregular time signatures, swing, guitar tab and chords, drum music, jazz chords, and tips for writing music down. Chapter 20 provides a brief history of musical notation.

At the end

The glossary (pages 119–138) provides short explanations of the terms used in this book and some others that you may encounter as a musician. And it refers to the pages where you can read about each subject in more detail. The last few pages of the book include a list of the major and minor scales, a do-it-yourself scale wheel and some handy memory aids.

Keyboard instruments

Pianos and keyboards are excellent instruments to demonstrate musical concepts, because every note has its own key, and because the keyboard is arranged in a clear pattern of black and white notes. In this book, many of the basics ideas are demonstrated on diagrams of a keyboard. To fully understand the explanations you'll need to have some kind of keyboard instrument – it doesn't matter if you don't know how to play it, and even the most basic model will do. You should be able to pick one up for as lit-tle as $25.

Styles of music

There are many systems of musical theory and notation around the world. This book only deals with Western music, but covers a great number of styles from classical music to rock, pop and jazz. Some of the examples used are nursery rhymes – this isn't because the book is aimed at small children, but because they are familiar to everyone and musically very simple.

Compositions and songs

A piece of classical music is usually called a *composition*, whilst in other styles the words most commonly used are *song*, *tune* or *number*. In this book, the neutral term *piece* is used in most cases, for compositions in any style of music.

2. NOTES AND MEASURES

This chapter shows you how to read basic rhythm. It introduces the various types of notes, each of which lasts for a different amount of time, and deals with beats, measures and time signatures.

With most styles of music you can tap your foot in time to what you hear. This is because music usually has a repetitive in-built *beat* or *pulse* at the root of its rhythm. For most music the symbol for a note that lasts one beat is this:

Notes that look like this are called *quarter notes*. Sometimes the beat is not a quarter note, but don't worry about that for now.

Counting
When you're learning to understand and read rhythm, it's essential to have some system of counting. For now we'll be counting in quarter-note beats – tap the following notes at an even pace and count the numbers out loud or in your head.

| 1 | 2 | 3 | 4 |

Bah Bah Black Sheep
In some music each note of the tune lasts one beat. Think,

for example, of the beginning of the nursery rhyme *Bah Bah Black Sheep*. If you sing the tune and tap the beat with your foot, you'll sing one note every time you tap one beat.

More notes

Obviously, most music is not this simple. Try singing the next line of *Bah Bah Black Sheep* ('Have you any wool') whilst tapping the beat with your foot. You'll notice that there is no longer one syllable to each beat. So we need more symbols to indicate notes of different length.

Count the beats

The following examples introduce the other basic notes. Above each example you'll see the numbers 1, 2, 3, 4 – this marks where the quarter-note beats are. Tap and count the beats, as you did before, and play each note on a random key on the keyboard. Don't play too fast.

The whole note: four quarter notes

The longest note that is regularly used in music is the *whole note*, which lasts as long as four quarter notes. If you play a whole note on a keyboard, you hold the key down for four quarter-note beats. On a wind instrument, you keep blowing for four quarter-note beats.

The whole note

The half note: two quarter notes

The *half note* lasts as longs as two quarter-note beats – half as long as a whole note.

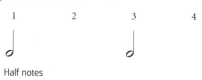

Half notes

The eighth note: half of a quarter note

The *eighth note* lasts half as long as the quarter note. So for every quarter-note beat you should play two evenly spaced notes – one at the same time as you tap your foot, the other as you lift it. Insert the word 'and' between the numbers to help you keep count.

Eighth notes

The sixteenth note: quarter of a quarter note

There are four *sixteenth notes* to each quarter-note beat – they sound twice as fast as eighth notes. To help you count these, try inserting 'ee' and 'a', as shown.

Sixteenth notes

Heads, stems and tails

A note consists of up to three components: a *head* (the round bit), a *stem* (the vertical line), and *tails* or *flags* (the

The note		Quarter notes
○	The whole note – open head	four
♩ (half note symbol)	The half note – open head and a stem	two
♩	The quarter note – closed head and a stem	one
♪	The eighth note – closed head, a stem and a tail	half
♬ (sixteenth note symbol)	The sixteenth note – closed head, a stem and two tails	quarter

7

short lines at the end of the stem). As you've probably noticed, the more 'bits' a note has, the less time it lasts for.

GROUPS OF NOTES

When rhythm is written down as a series of separate notes, one after the other, it can be hard to follow. To make things clearer, notes can be joined together into groups. In this situation, their tails become horizontal *beams*.

Beams = tails

As the following example shows, a beam has the same effect as a tail. An eighth note has one tail, so two eighth notes are joined together by one beam. Sixteenth notes have two tails, so are joined with two beams.

Mixed groups

Sixteenth notes and eighth notes can be grouped together. To help you read the rhythms, count 'one-ee-and-a' at a regular speed as you did when counting sixteenth notes.

Beams and beats

Notice that each of the groups written above is equal to one quarter-note beat in total. When these groups are used, the first note of each group always falls on the beat, making everything clearer. In the example below, you can see how the use of groups turns a confusing series of symbols into three bite-sized chunks. And because these same groups occur regularly in music, you quickly learn to recognize them, allowing you to play the correct rhythms without having to think about it.

Separate

With groups

Longer and shorter groups
Sometimes you'll see groups of two beats or half a beat, but the meaning is clear. For example:

Fewer beams for singers
Arranging words underneath groups of notes can be awkward, so music for singers often has each note written separately.

Other notes and groups
There are lots of other kinds of notes and ways to group notes together. These will be discussed later.

LEARN THE NOTE VALUES
Being able to quickly tell the length of a note – its *note value* – is very important when reading music. To get used to the five symbols introduced so far, look at the table overleaf, which shows these notes in relation to each other. Each line lasts the same amount of time: 1 whole note = 2 half notes = 4 quarter notes = 8 eighth notes = 16 sixteenth notes.

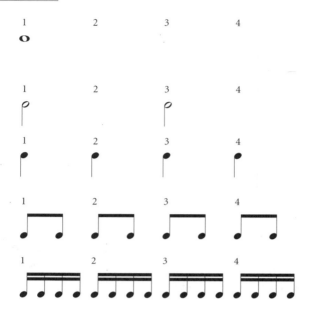

Even shorter notes

The shortest note mentioned so far is the sixteenth note, but there are even shorter ones. *Thirty-second notes* are quite common, but *sixty-fourth notes* are less so.

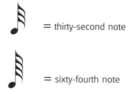

= thirty-second note

= sixty-fourth note

MEASURES

We've already noted that most music has a steady beat running through it. However, some beats have more of a natural emphasis than others. Sing *Bah Bah Black Sheep* again and notice how you naturally highlight the first beat of every four.

> **Bah** bah black sheep
> **Have** you any wool
> **Yes** sir yes sir
> **Three** bags full

In music

This natural cycle of four beats is represented when the music is written down. On paper, *Bah Bah Black Sheep* is broken up into four-beat sections – known as *measures* or *bars* – by thin vertical lines, called *bar lines*.

Bah   bah   black   sheep   have   you   a - ny   wool

TIME SIGNATURES

The particular way that a piece is divided up into measures is indicated by a *time signature*. The time signature is written at the beginning of a piece of music, and consists of two numbers, one on top of the other. Basically, the bottom number tells you what type of note is the beat, and the top number tells you how many beats there are in each measure.

A four at the bottom

Most commonly you'll see a four at the bottom of a time signature. This means that each beat is a quarter note long, as it has been so far in this chapter.

Four-four

The time signature of *Bah Bah Black Sheep* is the most common time signature of all: 4/4 (pronounced 'four-four'). Four-four is so frequently used that it's also referred to as *common time*. A measure in this time signature can be full of any combination of notes that adds up to four quarter notes – in this example the first measure contains four quarter notes, and the second measure contains eighth notes and a half note that add up to the same overall time.

Bah   bah   black   sheep   have   you   a - ny   wool

Three-four and two-four

Another commonly used time signature is 3/4 ('three-four'). As you can tell from the numbers, music in three-four has three beats in each measure, and each beat is a quarter note. 2/4 has two quarter-note beats in each measure (it can sound very similar to four-four).

A two at the bottom

If there's a two at the bottom of a time signature, such as in $\frac{2}{2}$, it means that the beats are counted in half notes instead of quarter notes. A measure in two-two lasts the same amount of time as a measure in four-four, but is counted differently. As you can see in the following example, a measure of two-two can include four quarter notes, but each is now counted as only half a beat.

An eight at the bottom

If there's an eight at the bottom of a time signature, it implies that eighth notes are the beat – so a measure of $\frac{3}{8}$ contains three eighth-note beats. In this time signature, three eighth notes are grouped together, as shown below.

Other time signatures

Some time signatures with an eight at the bottom, such as $\frac{6}{8}$ and $\frac{9}{8}$, are counted differently. This is explained in Chapter 5.

𝄴 and 𝄵

Instead of $\frac{4}{4}$, the symbol 𝄴 is sometimes used. It means exactly the same thing, and comes from an ancient way of writing time signatures. You may also see the symbol 𝄵, which is another way of indicating the $\frac{2}{2}$ time signature, which is also known as *alla breve* or *cut common time*.

British names

Notes are also known by their British names: *breve* (whole note), *minim* (half note), *crotchet* (quarter note), *quaver* (eighth note), *semiquaver* (sixteenth note).

3. HIGH AND LOW

All sound is caused by vibration: a guitar's strings vibrate, a trumpeter's lips vibrate, and if you sing or talk your vocal chords vibrate. A change in the speed of the vibration changes the pitch – how high or low the note sounds. This chapter explains how different pitches are written down.

The faster something vibrates, the higher the note sounds. The higher you sing, the faster your vocal chords vibrate. The shorter you make a guitar string, by pressing it to the frets, the faster it will vibrate, and the higher the note will be. The higher the key that you press on an electronic keyboard, the faster the speakers will vibrate.

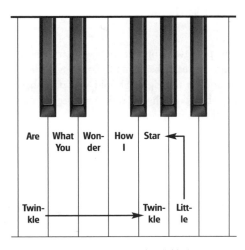

Twinkle Twinkle Little Star – each syllable is a note.

On a keyboard

On a keyboard or piano, the notes get higher as you move to the right. Using the diagram on the previous page, try playing *Twinkle Twinkle Little Star* – play each word on the key that it's written on. As you move to the right the notes get higher. As you go back to the left (after the word 'little') they get lower.

The octave

If you look at a keyboard or piano, then you can see a clear pattern of black and white notes. The pattern repeats after twelve notes, seven of which are white and five of which are black. If you start on any note and count up twelve notes, you'll arrive at the same point in the pattern that you started. In musical terms, the note you finished up on is an *octave* higher than the one you started on.

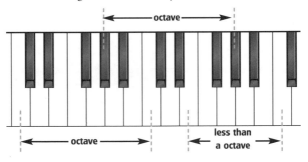

Octaves on a keyboard

Blending in

When you play two notes an octave apart, one after the other, you will clearly hear that the one on the left is lower than the one on the right. Should you play them at the same time, however, they blend in with each other – almost as if there's only one note.

Twice as fast

The reason they blend in with each other so well is scientific: when two notes are an octave apart, the higher note vibrates exactly twice as fast as the lower note. If you learnt Do–Re–Mi–Fa–So–La–Ti–Do at school, and you sing the first and last Do, the second one is one octave higher than the first, so your vocal chords vibrate twice as fast when you sing it.

The white keys

So, every octave is made up of twelve notes, or *pitches*. The white notes all have a letter name: C, D, E, F, G, A and B. These notes are called *naturals*, *natural notes*, or simply *white notes*.

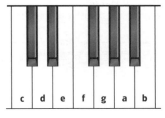

The seven naturals

Middle C

The note in the middle of a piano or keyboard is called *middle C*. This note is used as a kind of landmark, to help describe where other notes are – you could describe a note as 'the E above middle C', for example, or 'the C two octaves above middle C'.

Whole tones and half-tones

If you go from key to key on the keyboard, including black and white notes, each note is one *half-tone* higher or lower. Half-tones are also called *half-steps* and *semitones*. If you always skip one key (black or white) you will be playing steps of *whole tones*, or *tones*.

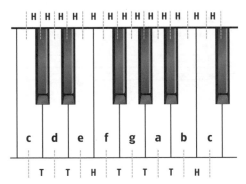

Whole tones (T) and half-tones (H)

Other instruments

Few instruments can play as many different octaves as a piano or a big keyboard, but all instruments use the same system of octaves, half-tones and tones. On a guitar, for example, each time you move your finger up one fret, the note rises by a half-tone. Each time you move your finger

15

up two frets, the note rises by a tone. And if you go up twelve frets, the note rises by an octave.

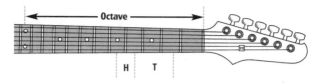

Whole tones (T), half-tones (H) and octaves on the guitar

THE STAVE

Music is written on a *stave* (or *staff*), which is a set of five horizontal lines. You count them from the bottom up, so the top line is the fifth line. You read and play the notes from left to right, just like words, and the higher a note is written on the stave, the higher it sounds.

Twinkle Twinkle on the stave

The following example shows *Twinkle Twinkle* on the stave. As the melody rises, the notes get higher, and when the tune falls (from the word 'little'), so do the notes.

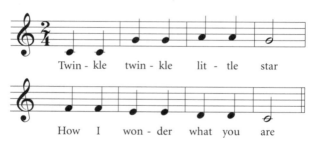

Lines and spaces

A note can be written on the stave in two ways:
• on a line (with the line running through the note).
• in the space between two lines, or below or above the lines.

Notes on the lines

Notes between, below and above the lines

Eleven notes

This way, eleven notes can be fitted onto the stave.

Eleven notes on the stave

Which line is which note?

You don't know which lines and spaces represent which notes until you've seen a *clef*. A clef is a symbol that specifies the note of one line – and once you know what that line represents you also know what all the others represent. Only two clefs are very common, one for high notes, the *treble clef*, and one for low notes, the *bass clef*.

The treble clef

The treble clef, which is shown below, is also called the *G clef*. This is because it specifies the second line of the stave as the G above middle C. This G is located a little to the right of the middle of a piano keyboard. The treble clef is used for high-sounding instruments such as violins and trumpets.

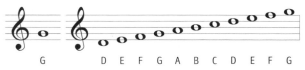

G   D E F G A B C D E F G

The treble clef or G clef

The bass clef

The bass clef, shown below, is also called the *F clef*, because it specifies the fourth line of the stave as the F below middle C. This F is located a little to the left of the middle of a piano keyboard. The bass clef is used for low-sounding instruments, such as the trombone and cello.

F   F G A B C D E F G A B

The bass clef or F clef

Ledger lines

So that more notes can be fitted on each stave, little extra lines can be added, which are called *ledger lines*. Each note on a ledger line has its own line or lines – they aren't joined up.

17

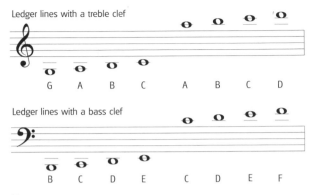

Ledger lines with a treble clef

G A B C A B C D

Ledger lines with a bass clef

B C D E C D E F

Two staves

Most instruments have their music written on one stave, but keyboard music is written on two. Usually the notes played by the right hand are written on the upper stave (with a treble clef) and the notes played by the left hand are written on the lower stave (with a bass clef).

Right hand:

Left hand:

Notes and keys

The diagram below shows where the notes of a piano or keyboard lie on the stave. You can see that middle C is 'in

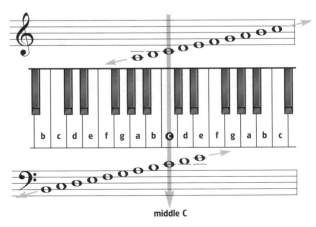

b c d e f g a b c d e f g a b c

middle C

between' the bass and the treble staves: it's written one ledger line below the treble stave and one ledger line above the bass stave.

Other clefs

The treble and bass clefs are not the only ones – indeed at one time many different clefs were used. Today, however, the only other clef you're likely to come across is the *alto clef* or *C clef*. This is the clef usually used for viola music, because the range of the viola lies equally in the bass and treble clefs. In this clef, middle C is in the middle of the stave, on the third line.

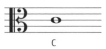

The C clef sets the third line as middle C

Changing clefs

Many instruments have all their music written in one clef. A flute player, for example, will never come across any clef other than the treble clef. However, some instruments have a range that goes from low to high, so they need to make use of more than one type of clef. The left hand of the piano, for example, usually plays quite low notes, and so is written in the bass clef. But if there's a very high passage, the music simply changes into the treble clef, as shown in the example below. In the same way, the right hand can go into the bass clef.

Sometimes the clef changes

Very high and low

A problem arises when a passage of music needs to be written very high above the treble clef or very low below the bass clef. As we've seen, ledger lines extend the stave up and down, but if notes are written on more than three or four ledger lines, reading can get quite difficult.

19

The solution is simple – when a note or passage is written far above the treble clef or far below the bass clef, the player is told to play an octave higher or lower than what's actually written.

8va

The symbol *8va*, or *8*, is written above the first note that you have to play an octave higher, as shown in the example below. If you're required to play an octave lower, one of the following symbols is written under the first note: *8va bassa*, *8vb*, *8va*, or *8*. If the 8 is replaced by a 15 in any of these markings, you play *two* octaves higher or lower.

Two ways of writing the same melody, the one below using the 8va sign to avoid lots of ledger lines.

For how long?

From the marking, there's usually a line to show you how long to continue playing one octave higher or lower (as in the above example). If there's no line, you keep playing an octave higher or lower until you see the word *loco*.

Transposing instruments

Many wind instruments are so-called *transposing instruments*, which means the notes they produce are different from the notes they read. For example, when a tenor saxophonist reads an A, they actually produce a G. Transposing instruments and transposition are explained in Chapter 16. Non-transposing instruments are said to play in *concert pitch*.

Always 8va

Some instruments have all their music written one octave lower or higher, but these aren't considered to be transposing instruments – a C on such an instrument is still a C, it's just a different C. Music for guitar, double bass and bass guitar, for example, is all written an octave higher than it actually sounds, whilst music for the piccolo is written an octave lower.

CHORDS

Two or more notes played at the same time form a *chord*. On paper, the notes of a chord are aligned vertically – here are some examples:

Chords are written as 'piles' of notes

Adjacent notes

If a chord includes two notes which occupy adjacent places on the stave – such as a D and an E – the notes don't fit exactly one on top of the other, but you still play them at the same time. Here are two examples:

Adjacent notes in a chord don't fit exactly one on top of the other

Chords and numbers

You can read more about chords, and how they are sometimes abbreviated with letters and numbers, on pages 111–112.

4. MORE ABOUT RHYTHM

In Chapter 2 you learnt the basics about notes and measures. This chapter extends that knowledge, introducing rests, triplets, dots, ties and compound time.

In every example so far, each measure has been full of notes. However, music also contains silences, which are indicated on paper by rests. Just like notes, there are many types of *rests*, each of which lasts a different length of time. Conveniently, they share the same names as notes of the equivalent lengths.

Rests

Just like the whole note, the *whole rest* lasts for four quarter-note beats. This rest looks like a small block hanging from the fourth line on the stave. The *half-note rest* is the

symbol	name	lasts as long as		no. of quarter notes
	whole rest		whole note	four
	half rest		half note	two
	quarter rest		quarter note	one
	eighth rest		eighth note	half
	sixteenth rest		sixteenth note	quarter

same block, but it lies on top of the third line. (Some people find it useful to remember that the rest which lasts longer is 'heavier' and therefore hangs down.) The quarter rest is unlike the other signs, but the symbols for eighth and sixteenth rests are similar to the equivalent notes in that every extra tail halves the length.

The whole measure rest

A measure is always full of the correct total amount of notes and rests. However, regardless of the time signature, a whole measure's rest is always indicated by a whole rest.

Multiple measures

Sometimes you may be required to remain quiet for more than one measure at a time. There is a special symbol for this situation, which saves composers the space and effort of writing out lots of measures with a whole rest in, and makes long rests easier to count. The symbol is written in just one measure and has the required number of measures' rest written above it. Below is an example of a sixteen-measure rest.

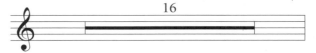

A sixteen-measure rest

DOTS AND TIES

You've seen the symbols that represent certain lengths for notes and rests. However, notes of other lengths, such as three beats, or one and a half beats, can also be written down – with *dots* and *ties*.

Dots

One way a note can be made longer is by the addition of a dot. A dot makes a note one and a half times longer.

2 + 1 = 3

A half note lasts two quarter-note beats, so a *dotted half note* lasts one and a half times that, which is three quarter-note beats. A quarter note lasts one quarter-note beat, so a *dotted quarter note* lasts one and a half quarter-note beats.

3 beats (2 + 1)   **1½ beats (1 + ½)**   **¾ beat (½ + ¼)**

Adding a dot makes a note last one and a half times as long

My Country 'Tis of Thee

My Country 'Tis of Thee is an example of a tune with dotted quarter note.

| 1 | 2 | 3 | 1 | 2 | and | 3 |

My   count - try   'tis   of   thee

Beams

Dotted notes with tails can be beamed into groups just like other notes. Here are some examples — notice how they still add up to a quarter note in total.

1   ee   and   **a**

1   **ee**   and   a

Two dots

You may occasionally come across a note with two dots, in which case the second dot adds half of what the first one adds. Thus, a double-dotted half note lasts two + one + a half quarter-note beats, which equals three and a half. Double-dotted notes, though, aren't very common.

Dotted rests

Rests can be dotted in exactly the same way as notes. A quarter rest with a dot, for example, tells you to be silent for one and a half quarter-note beats.

A dotted quarter rest lasts one and a half beats. A dotted eighth rest lasts three-quarters of a beat.

Ties

A *tie* extends a note by joining it to another note of the same pitch. If two notes are *tied*, the second note is simply held on, instead of being played separately.

Each of the tied pairs sounds like one note

Slurs

It's important not to get ties muddled up with slurs, which look the same but connect notes of different pitch. *Slurs* are explained in Chapter 8.

Sounds the same

Many rhythms can be written with either a dotted note or a slur. For example, the two figures below sound exactly the same.

What's the difference?

Dotted notes are usually easier to read than tied notes, so they are normally used wherever possible. However, there are things that can be done only with ties, such as extending a note 'over' a bar line, and creating a note of any length.

Creating an unusual note length (seven and a half beats), by tying a note 'over' the bar line

THE FIRST AND LAST MEASURES

As you've seen, measures are always completely full. In a four-four piece, every measure contains a combination of notes and rests that adds up to the same value as four quarter notes. In a three-four measure, all the notes and rests together last exactly as long as three quarter notes.

One exception

One exception to this rule is the very first measure of a piece, which is often shorter than the time signature would suggest. Many compositions begin with a little lead-in to the first full measure. The note or series of notes in this shortened first measure is called the *upbeat* (a word which derives from the motion of a conductor's baton). Other terms for the upbeat are *anacrusis* (a classical term) and *pickup* (a non-classical term).

Hap - py   birth - day   to   you   Hap - py...

Happy Birthday has an upbeat

The final measure

If a piece starts with an upbeat, the length of the first and last measures will usually add up to one whole measure. For example, if a piece in four-four has an upbeat of one beat, the final measure will usually only have three beats.

TRIPLETS AND OTHER -PLETS

So far, notes have always been divided by factors of two: wholes, halves, quarters, eighths, and so on. But notes can also be divided in lots of other ways.

Triplets

If you divide a quarter note in half you get two eighth notes. If you divide it into three, you get a *triplet*, or, more accurately, an *eighth-note triplet*. A triplet is very easy to recognize as it has a number 3 written above or below the notes, sometimes with a square bracket or curved line.

Three ways of writing an eighth-note triplet

Counting

An eighth-note triplet tells you to play three evenly spaced notes in the time it takes to play one quarter note. Try counting these as 'Mex-i-co, Mex-i-co', etc.

Mex – i – co   Mex – i – co   Mex – i – co   Mex – i – co

Quarter-note triplets

A *quarter-note triplet* is three notes in the space of one half note. These take a bit of practice to get right.

Quarter-note triplets: three notes in the space of one half note

Sixteenth-note triplets

A *sixteenth-note triplet* is formed by dividing an eighth note into three – you play three evenly spaced notes in the time it would normally take to play one eighth note. These triplets are often combined with 'regular' eighth notes, as shown below.

Two common combinations: an eighth note followed by a sixteenth-note triplet, and vice versa.

Not always all three

You don't always play all three notes of a triplet. Below are some eighth-note triplets with a note missing:

Mex – i – **co**   **Mex** – **i** – co   Mex – **i** – **co**

Longer notes

Sometimes two notes in a triplet (usually the first and second) are played as a single note. In this case you only hear two notes but there's no rest in between. This can be written in two ways:

27

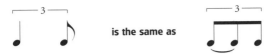

is the same as

Two ways to indicate a triplet with only the first and third notes played

Other variations

The individual notes within a triplet can be dotted or sub-divided just like any other notes.

The notes within a triplet can be dotted or subdivided

Sextuplets

If you play six notes in the space of one, you get a *sextuplet*. The example below shows a sixteenth-note sextuplet: six notes played in the space of one quarter note. This sounds the same as two sixteenth-note triplets one after the other.

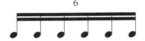

A sextuplet: six notes played in the space of one quarter note

Antimetric

Triplets are *antimetric* figures. They tend to feel like they're going 'against the rhythm', sounding noticeably different from notes divided into twos, fours, etc. There are many other antimetric figures, which you'll see much less frequently, such as the *quintuplet* (five evenly spaced notes played in the time it usually takes to play one note) and *septuplet* (seven evenly spaced notes played in the time it usually takes to play one note). Quintuplets or septuplets joined with two beams are required to fit into the space of a quarter note; if they are joined by a single beam they are required to fit into the space of a half note.

A quintuplet the length of a quarter note and a septuplet the length of a half note

METER AND COMPOUND TIME

The *meter* of a piece of music refers to the number of beats in a measure, and is represented by the time signature. *Quadruple meter* means there are four beats in a measure (such as in $\frac{4}{4}$), *triple meter* means there are three (such as in $\frac{3}{4}$), and *duple meter* means there are two (such as in $\frac{2}{4}$).

Simple time

All the time signatures discussed so far have been examples of *simple time*, which means that the beat has been a straightforward note such as a quarter note (for example in four-four) or a half note (for example in two-two).

Compound time

Compound time signatures have a dotted note for a beat. The most common compound time signature is $\frac{6}{8}$. As the numbers tell you, there are six eighth notes in a measure, but there are not six eighth-note beats – there are two dotted quarter-note beats. This may sound complicated but it's actually very simple.

Groups of three

Compound time signatures are used for tunes where the beat is always divided into three. This is because they have a dotted note as a beat, and dotted notes can be equally divided into three. The example below shows a melody in six-eight. You count two beats in each measure, and each beat consists of a group of three eighth notes, or notes of the equivalent length.

A melody in $\frac{6}{8}$

Other compound meters

Basically, every time signature with a 6, 9 or 12 at the top is a compound time signature. $\frac{9}{8}$, for example, has three dotted quarter-note beats (*compound triple time*), $\frac{12}{8}$ has four dotted eighth note groups (*compound quadruple time*). Don't be worried if this all sounds very complicated – six-eight is the only compound time signature you're likely to come across very often, and if you see another, you can usually tell how to count it from the way that the notes are grouped together.

5. SHARPS AND FLATS

The naturals or white notes discussed in Chapter 3 are just seven of the twelve notes in each octave. This chapter looks at the black notes, and explains sharps and flats.

The black notes are named in relation to the white notes: if a black note is one half-tone higher than a white note it's called a *sharp*; if a black note is one half-tone lower than a white note it's called a *flat*.

Sharps

The black note one half-tone higher than G, for example, is called *G sharp*. Sharps are indicated with a sharp sign (♯), so a G sharp can be written as G♯. On the stave, the sharp sign appears before – and at the same height as – the note it relates to, so a G♯ is written like this:

G sharp or G♯

Flats

The black note one half-tone lower than G is called *G flat*. Flats are indicated with a flat sign (♭), so a G flat can be written as G♭. On the stave, the flat sign appears before – and at the same height as – the note it relates to, so a G♭ is written like this:

G flat or G♭

One note, two names

Every black note is between two white notes, one of which

is a half-tone higher and one of which is one half-tone lower. This means that every black note has two names. Two notes that sound the same, such as F♯ and G♭, are said to be *enharmonic*, or *enharmonic equivalents*.

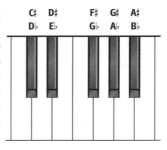

On the stave

So, on the stave each black note can appear in two ways – as a flat and as a sharp.

F sharp sounds the same as G flat, and they are played on the same key

White sharps and flats

Any natural note can be raised or lowered by a half-tone to make a sharp or flat – even when the resulting note is played on a white note. For example, if you lower a C by a half-tone you get a C♭, but one look at the keyboard shows you that the note one half-tone lower than C is B natural. So a C♭ sounds the same as a B. These are also enharmonic. There are four enharmonic pairs involving the white notes:

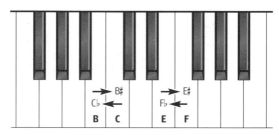

B♯ sounds the same as C, C♭ sounds the same as B, E♯ sounds the same as F and F♭ sounds the same as E

All the sharps

The following diagram shows all the sharps, both on the keyboard and the stave.

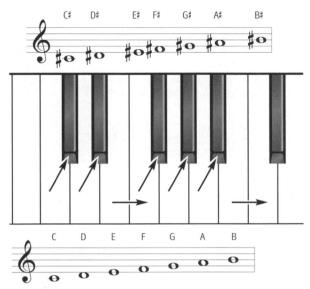

The natural notes and the sharps

All the flats

Below, all the flats are shown in the same way.

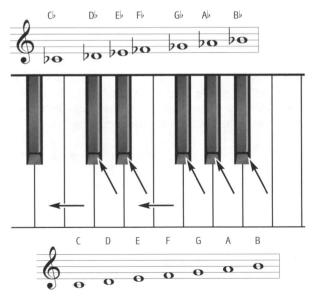

The natural notes and the flats

The natural sign

The natural sign (♮) returns a note altered by a sharp or flat to its natural position. Like the sharp and flat symbols it is written before – and at the same height as – the note it applies to. Exactly how and when the natural sign is used is explained in the following section.

B flat   B natural

KEY SIGNATURES

Sharps and flats are *chromatic symbols*. In many pieces a certain number of either sharps or flats appear at the beginning of each stave, just after the clef. However, sharps and flats can also appear at any point throughout a piece.

Key signatures

If one or more sharps or flats appear at the beginning of the stave, just after the clef, then these are the *key signature* of the piece. Any flats and sharps in the key signature apply to the whole piece: if there's a B flat in the key signature, every B in the entire piece is lowered to a B flat.

Some examples

In the first example shown below, the key signature consists of two sharps – F♯ and C♯. This means that every F and C, in any octave, is raised to F♯ or C♯. In the second example, the key signature contains three flats – B♭, E♭ and A♭ – so every B, E and A is flattened accordingly.

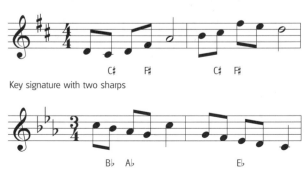

Key signature with two sharps

Key signature with three flats

Keys

As well as telling you which sharps or flats to play throughout the piece, the key signature tells you what *key* the piece is in. You don't necessarily need to know about keys to read music, but it makes it much easier, and gives you a greater insight into what you're playing. Chapters 11 to 15 deal with this subject.

More sharps or flats

Pieces of music can have key signatures with up to seven sharps or flats. However, with a bit of practice you won't need to look at every sharp or flat in a key signature to work out which notes to sharpen or flatten in a piece. The sharps and flats always appear in a fixed order, so if you know this order, a quick look at the number of sharps or flats is enough to tell you which notes to raise or lower.

Seven sharps

If there's just one sharp, it always raises each F to F♯. If there are two, they always sharpen every F and C; if there are three, they sharpen every F, C and G. This order continues, as shown on the diagram below, until a seventh sharp is added, raising every B to B♯. This is the maximum number of sharps in a key signature.

The key signature with seven sharps in the bass and treble clefs

Seven flats

A key signature with just one flat always flattens every B to

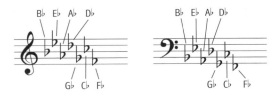

The key signature with seven flats in the bass and treble clefs

35

B♭. If there are two, they flatten every B and E; three flatten every B, E and A. Again, this order continues, as shown, until the seventh flat is added – the F♭.

From memory

It's good to learn these orders by heart – at least up to three or four flats and sharps. Then, if you see a piece in three flats, for example, you'll know immediately that you're supposed to lower all the Bs, Es and As. All this is explained in much more depth in Chapters 11 and 12.

ACCIDENTALS

Chromatic symbols don't appear only in the key signature. Sharps and flats – as well as natural signs – can also appear throughout a piece of music, raising and lowering particular notes. When they are used in this way they're called *accidentals*.

Until the end of the measure

Sharps and flats in the key signature apply to the whole piece. But accidentals only apply from where they are written until the end of the measure. So in the example below, the sharp sign turns both the Fs that follow it into F♯s, but it doesn't affect the F before it or the F in the next measure.

Accidentals apply from where they appear until the end of the measure

Only one pitch

Each accidental only alters notes of one particular pitch. In the example below, the natural sign before the first E doesn't apply to the second E in the measure, because it is a different pitch (an octave higher). So two accidentals are needed to naturalize both Es.

An accidental only applies to one pitch

Reminder accidentals

Sometimes a sharp, flat or natural sign is given just as a reminder: if it wasn't there, the music would be the same, but it's written anyway just to remind you to play the correct note. These *reminder accidentals* often appear in brackets.

Accidentals and ties

If a note written with an accidental is tied over a bar line, the accidental isn't written twice – the first one applies to both bits of the tied note. However, once the tied note is finished, the accidental no longer applies – so in the example below, a second sharp sign is needed.

An accidental applies throughout a tied note, but not to the whole of the next measure

FLAT OR SHARP?

If a note has two names – such as C♯ and D♭ – then how does a composer choose which note to write? It depends, for one thing, on the key signature of the piece. If you want to know more about keys, turn to Chapter 11.

Going up, going down

When it comes to accidentals, the direction of the melody is a major factor in choosing between two enharmonic notes. If the melody goes up, the composer is likely to go for a raised note; when the direction is downward, often a flat is used. In the following example, a G♯ and an A♭ (which sound the same) are both used in the space of two measures, because the direction of the melody changes.

Enharmonic notes, such as G♯ and A♭ in this example, sound the same but are used in different situations.

DOUBLE SHARPS AND FLATS

Doubly raised and lowered notes are not very common, but you may come across them occasionally. The double flat (♭♭) lowers the natural note by two half-tones. If a G is preceded by a double flat it is called a *G double-flat*, and it sounds the same as an F.

Double sharps

The double sharp has its own symbol: 𝄪. It makes a note two half-tones higher. If a G is preceded by a double sharp sign, then it becomes a *G double-sharp*, and it sounds the same as an A.

Why not an A?

What's the point in writing a G double-sharp if it sounds the same as an A? Because although they have the same sound, they are different notes and have different uses, just like the G♯ and A♭ in the example on page 37. Again, this will become much clearer once you learn about scales and keys.

6. LOUD AND SOFT

If you play every note at the same volume, you'll sound more like a machine than a musician. In some styles there's hardly any variation between loud and soft, but in most music changes in volume are very important.

In musical terms, variations in volume are called *dynamics*, and *dynamic markings* indicate how loud or soft you should play. Dynamics are usually indicated by Italian words or their abbreviations.

From soft to loud

The standard dynamic markings are shown below. Note that mezzo-piano is slightly softer than mezzo-forte.

Abbreviation	Meaning	Indicating
ppp	pianississimo	very, very soft
pp	pianissimo	very soft
p	piano	soft
mp	mezzo-piano	moderately soft
mf	mezzo-forte	moderately loud
f	forte	loud
ff	fortissimo	very loud
fff	fortississimo	very, very loud

Even louder, even softer

Occasionally, you may come across dynamic markings with four or even more letters (such as *ffff* or *ppppp*), which basically tell you to play as loud or as soft as possible. Obviously, how much noise you actually make depends on your instrument – *ff* on recorder may be quieter than *mp* on an electric guitar.

Until the next marking

These abbreviations are located under the first note they apply to. From that note onwards you keep playing at the indicated volume until you come across the next dynamic marking.

Getting louder

A *crescendo* ('growing' in Italian) is when you get gradually louder. A short crescendo, over just a few notes or measures, is usually indicated by two diverging lines ($\diagdown$). A longer one is often indicated by the word crescendo, or the abbreviation *cresc.*, followed by a dotted line, which shows how long the change in volume should last.

Getting softer

A *diminuendo* or *decrescendo* is when you gradually get quieter. Short diminuendos are usually indicated by two converging lines ($\diagup$), whilst longer ones, just like with crescendos, use a word (diminuendo, decrescendo, *dim.* or *decresc.*) followed by a dotted line.

Poco and molto

Sometimes you'll see a crescendo or diminuendo written with the term *poco a poco*. This means 'little by little' and tells you to get louder or softer very slowly. If a crescendo or diminuendo appears with the word *molto*, on the other hand, you should change the volume more intensely.

Read ahead

There's usually a dynamic marking after a crescendo or diminuendo, which tells you the volume you should be aiming for. It's important to read ahead so you can judge how much louder or softer you should be getting.

A crescendo from piano to forte

In English

In non-classical music, dynamics are often indicated in English. A songwriter might use anything from a simple 'loud' or 'soft' to terms such as 'screaming', which tell you not only to play at a certain volume, but also in a particular way.

Sudden changes

A note or chord marked *fp* (meaning *fortepiano*) should start with a loud 'burst' but then quickly drop in volume. A *sforzando* (*sfz* or *sf*) also tells you to play with sudden extra force, but with this marking the extra volume should last for the whole note or chord.

Accents

Because they only apply to one note or chord, fortepiano and sforzando are really types of accents. You will read about other types of accents in Chapter 8.

7. FAST AND SLOW

There are two main ways of indicating the speed, or tempo, of music – with numbers or Italian terms. Additionally, there are all sorts of words that indicate *how* a piece should be played.

The most precise way of indicating the speed of a piece is by stating the number of *beats per minute* (BPM). You will often find this indication at the top of the piece, with a note and a number, such as ♩ = **120**. This example tells you there should be 120 quarter notes in each minute.

Metronomes

A *metronome* is a clockwork or electronic device that helps you set and keep to the right tempo by providing a steady tick or beep. You can set the beats per minute on a

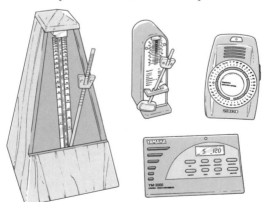

Two mechanical (wind-up) and two electronic metronomes

metronome – most have a range of roughly 40 to 208 BPM. Music written any slower than 40 BPM is extremely rare, and for really fast pieces, you can simply halve the metronome indication. For example, if the tempo is 240 BPM ($\downarrow$ = **240**), you can set your metronome to 120, and it will still keep you in time.

M.M.

The metronome was improved and patented by a man called Maelzel, and BPM indication are sometimes preceded by the letters M.M. This simply stands for 'Maelzel's Metronome', and doesn't change the meaning.

Italian terms

The other way to indicate tempo is with Italian words – these are used in both classical and non-classical music. Most metronomes show the common Italian terms, and show how they correspond to BPM. Here are some of the most common tempo markings, from slow to fast.

Italian term	Meaning	Metronome marking
Largo	very slow	$\downarrow$ = **40–60**
Adagio	slow	$\downarrow$ = **60–76**
Andante	walking pace	$\downarrow$ = **76–108**
Moderato	medium tempo	$\downarrow$ = **108–120**
Allegro	fast	$\downarrow$ = **120–168**
Presto	very fast	$\downarrow$ = **168–200**

Prestissimo and larghetto

Italian words indicating tempo or anything else sometimes appear with different endings. The suffix *-issimo*, for instance, means 'more than', whilst the suffix *-etto* means 'less than'. So *prestissimo* is faster than presto, implying a metronome marking of 200–208, and *larghetto* is a bit less slow than largo ($\downarrow$ = **60–66**).

Rubato

The word *rubato* tells you to play a piece or section quite 'freely', altering the rhythm slightly as you feel necessary to maximize the expression. This instruction, which is most commonly found in slow pieces, stems from the Italian word 'robbed' – you 'steal' a little time from one note or measure and add it to another.

Tempo changes

Most pieces are played at the same tempo from beginning to end. Although it's often up to either a drummer or conductor to keep the tempo steady, it's a good idea to practice with a metronome from time to time to develop your own timing skills. If the tempo is meant to change – if it slows down at the end, for example – then obviously you shouldn't practice that section with a metronome.

Slowing down and speeding up

There are also Italian terms that tell you to gradually slow down or speed up.

- *Accelerando* (*accel.*) and *stringendo* (*string.*) indicate that the tempo should increase.
- If you have to slow down, you'll read *ritenuto* (*rit.* or *riten.*), *rallentando* (*rall.*) or *ritardando* (*ritard.*).
- *Allargando* is another way of telling you to slow down. Literally, it means 'broadening out', and it can be interpreted as indicating a crescendo as well as a decrease in speed.
- *A Tempo* or *Tempo I °* (pronounced *Tempo Primo*) tells you to return to the original tempo.

Gradually

All these terms imply that you should change speed gradually rather than suddenly, but, just as with changes of volume, the words *poco a poco* (little by little) are added if the change should be very gradual.

Ad libitum

Ad libitum (*ad lib.*) means 'at liberty', implying that it's up to you what you do. It often refers to the tempo, but it may also have another, or a much broader, meaning. For example, *8va ad lib.* means you are free to play the marked section an octave higher – but you don't have to.

English

Of course, English, or any other language, can be used to indicate tempo, and terms such as 'fast', *ballad* or *up tempo* are becoming ever more common.

MOOD AND TEMPO

Although there are no hard and fast rules, there's obviously a relationship between tempo and mood – melancholy tunes and tender love songs are normally quite slow, whilst feel-good and dance music is generally faster. Not surprisingly, then, some terms that imply a particular mood also imply a certain tempo.

Terms

Some of the commonest terms for mood are shown below. Sometimes these appear alongside a BPM indication, but often you just have to pick a tempo suitable for the mood. There are many more terms than those listed below (in Italian and other languages).

agitato	agitated
con brio	with brilliance
con fuoco	with fire
con spirito	with spirit or vigor
dolce	sweetly
tranquillo	with tranquillity
vivace	lively

Very, more, less

It's also worth knowing the following Italian words, which are often combined with terms already mentioned.

assai	very or sufficiently
molto	very
meno	less
(ma) non troppo	(but) not too much
più	more
un poco	a little, a bit
e	and

Combinations

These words can appear in any combination, such as *un poco più presto*, which tells you to start playing a little faster. Usually the combinations are short, but occasionally you may come across an instruction as long as *poco a poco stringendo e crescendo ma non troppo* (gradually get a little faster and a bit louder, but not too much).

8. ARTICULATION

Just as with words, you can 'pronounce' or articulate notes in many different ways – from dry and incisive to round and lingering. A variety of symbols, including dots, slurs and v-like signs, are used to indicate different types of articulation.

One common articulation sign is the *accent*, which instructs you to play a particular note or chord with extra force. Accents are written with a > sign above or below each note.

Accents: give notes extra emphasis

Even louder

Notes with a ∧ sign above or below them are played with even more volume and attack than those with a normal accent. If there is a dot inside the ∧ sign, the notes have to be played short as well as loud.

More intense accents: even more emphasis

Staccato

Notes with a dot above or below them are to be played *staccato* – short and clipped. Remember, though, a staccato quarter note may not last as long as a regular one, but it takes up as much time in the music. Sometimes, instead of every note having a dot, a passage is marked with the word staccato.

Staccato: shorten the note

Staccatissimo

If there's a small triangle, instead of a dot, the notes should be played *staccatissimo* – even shorter than staccato.

Staccatissimo: extra short

Slurs and legato

Legato (literally 'bound') is the opposite of staccato. When music is played legato, the notes are held on slightly longer than usual so there is no gap between them. *Slurs* are the curved lines used to show legato, binding notes together into groups. If you're a string player, you should play notes that are bound by a slur in a single bowing action.

Legato: the notes are smoothly 'bound together'

Phrase mark

Not every curvy line is a legato slur. The *phrase mark* looks similar but has a different meaning. In a similar way to

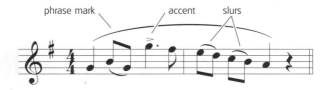

The phrase mark: shows a 'musical sentence'

how words are arranged into sentences, music is arranged into phrases, and phrase marks show where these phrases lie. If you are a wind player or a singer, you play or sing a phrase in one breath. You may find other markings, including slurs, within a phrase, as shown in the example on the previous page.

Tenuto

Another type of accent is the *agogic accent,* or *tenuto,* which is indicated by a horizontal line over or under the note. A note with an agogic accent is 'leaned on': held on for its full duration and often played with a little extra volume.

Tenuto: extend the notes slightly

Marcato

The term *marcato* means 'marked'. If a passage of music has this word written above it, you should play every note a little louder and shorter than usual.

Simile

The word similar stems from the Italian word *simile.* In music, simile tells you to continue a certain way of playing. Printed after a few staccato notes, for instance, it means that all the notes that follow are to be played staccato.

Fermata

A *fermata,* or *pause,* tells you to hold a note or chord for longer than it's actually written. Exactly how long you hold it for is a mater of taste – it's up to you in a solo piece, or to the conductor, leader or drummer in an orchestra or group. Fermata signs are often found at the end of pieces.

Fermata: hold for as long as you feel necessary

Arpeggio

An arpeggio sign tells you to 'spread' a chord out – introduce the notes one by one.

The arpeggio sign: spreads a chord out

Pizzicato

Some articulation signs only apply to particular instruments. *Pizzicato*, or *pizz.*, for example, is used for string instruments (violin, viola, cello, double bass), telling the player to pluck the strings with their fingers instead of bowing them.

Other markings

As you'd expect, there are many other articulation markings – some composers even invent their own and put a key to explain them at the beginning, and some symbols are only used in a particular musical style.

JAZZ AND FUSION

Jazz and fusion are mainly American in origin, so the articulation markings are usually named in English. Some examples are shown below.

Scoop

A *scoop* is when you briefly bend the pitch of a note downward, not more than a half-tone. Scoops are most commonly found in sax parts.

The scoop: briefly bend the pitch

Du and wah

The *du-wah* is mainly used by brass players. The 'du', a plus sign above a note, means you should smother the sound, by putting your hand or a *plunger* (a type of mute) in front of the bell of the instrument. The 'wah', a small circle, tells you to play the note *open*, without the hand or plunger. Harmonica players produce a similar effect with their hands, and guitarists with a *wah-wah* pedal.

Du and wah: muted and open

Ghost notes

A *ghost note* is a dead-sounding note with a hardly defin-able pitch. Most instruments have a specific technique for making these notes: wind players can make them with their tongue, guitarists by damping the strings, and so on.

The ghost note: dead-sounding

9. ORNAMENTS

In music, ornaments are decorative notes that embellish the main notes. This chapter introduces the most common ones, from trills to turns, and gives a guide to how to play them. The exact rhythm of each, though, can change depending on speed and taste.

Perhaps the best-known ornament is the *trill*, or *shake*, which is played by alternating very fast between the *main* or *principal* note and the note above it, the *upper note*. A trill can begin either on the principal note or the upper note.

Notation: Is played:

The trill

The mordent

There are two sorts of mini-trills, called *mordents*. The *upper mordent* tells you to trill just once to the upper note.

Notation: Is played:

The upper mordent: a one-note trill to the upper note

The inverted mordent

The inverted mordent, predictably enough, tells you to trill once on the note below the principal note (the *lower note*).

Notation: Is played:

The inverted mordent: a one-note trill to the lower note

Sharps, flats and trills

Trills and mordents are played on the note above or below the principal note in the key signature that you're in – sharps and flats remain valid. Only if a flat, sharp or natural sign appears above or below the sign must you lower, raise or naturalize the upper or lower note.

Notation: Is played:

Mordent with the upper note flattened from E to E♭

Tremolo

Tremolo is a quick repetition of one note, or a fast alternation between two notes.

Notation: Is played:

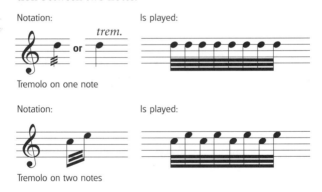

Tremolo on one note

Notation: Is played:

Tremolo on two notes

Vibrato

A note played with *vibrato* oscillates slightly but quickly in pitch. Guitarists, violinists and other string players rapidly move their finger backward and forward a tiny distance on the string to create vibrato. Wind players change the tension of the muscles in and around their mouth to adjust the air stream, and many keyboards and synthesizers have a *modulation* button/wheel, which simulates the effect.

There is no standard symbol for vibrato, because it's used to some extent by all good players in most styles of music. Occasionally, though, you may come across the abbreviation *vib.*, which instructs you to play that note with extra vibrato, or *non-vib.*, which tells you to play without any vibrato.

Vibrato or tremolo?

Vibrato and *tremolo* often get mixed up. The small arm (the *whammy bar*) found on many electric guitars, for example, is often called the *tremolo arm*, but in fact it can't be used to play tremolo. It can be used to play vibrato, by quickly moving the arm up and down over a very small distance, and *pitch bend*, by moving the arm once over a larger distance.

Grace notes

A *grace note* is a small, crossed-out note, placed just before a normal note. You can play it in two ways: just before the beat on which the main note falls, or exactly on the beat, in which case the main note comes fractionally later. The first way is more common. The Italian name for grace note is *acciaccatura*.

The grace note: a short note preceding the principal note

Appoggiaturas

Appoggiaturas look very similar to grace notes, but they don't have a line through them. An appoggiatura is played

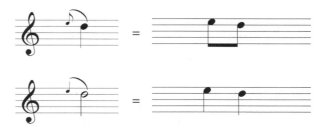

The appoggiatura: takes up about half the time of the note it precedes

on the beat of the normal-sized note it precedes, and takes up about half of its time.

The turn

A *turn* or *gruppetto* tells you to play a particular pattern of notes around the main note. As you can see below, the pattern of the symbol is similar to the pattern of notes.

Notation: Is played:

The turn: playing around the main note

The turn between two notes

You may also come across a turn symbol between two notes. In this case you play a similar pattern but end on the second note, as shown below.

Notation: Is played:

Three extra notes between two main notes

The glissando

A *glissando* is when a player slides from one note to another. The way that it's played, obviously, depends on the instrument: on a trombone you use the slide, on a piano you sweep your fingertips over the keys, and on a string instrument you slide your fingers up or down the string. Most electronic keyboards have a *pitch bend* control, which offers an electronic equivalent of the glissando.

The glissando: a slide from note to note

Fall, lift, plop and doit

A *glissando* indicates a starting note and an end note. *Falls, lifts, plops* and *doits*, which are ornaments mainly used in jazz, only show one or the other. The direction and length of the markings usually suggest how, and how far, you should slide.

The fall, or fall off: falling down from a note

The lift: rising up from a note

The plop: falling into a note

The doit: a short upward bend of a note

And more

There are plenty of other ornament signs and symbols. With the knowledge of the ones in this chapter, though, you'll usually be able to figure out how to play them when you see them.

10. SECTION MARKINGS AND REPEAT SIGNS

Compositions usually consist of a number of different sections, such as the verses and choruses that make up most songs. Often, you need to repeat a section a number of times, or skip backwards or forwards to a particular point. To save whole sections being written out more than once there are a number of special markings and signs which act like signposts, directing you around a piece of music.

As well as verses and choruses, there are plenty of other names for the various parts of a piece of music. In terms of songs, the word *intro* refers to the first section, before a number really gets going – usually the bit before the vocals come in. The term *outro* is often used for the final section, when the singing has stopped, and a *bridge* literally bridges two different sections – you'll find one at the letter B in *Take the 'A' Train*, at the end of this chapter.

Classical terms

There is also a whole array of names for the sections of classical pieces, from *exposition* (an opening section) and *recapitulation* (a return to the opening), to *interlude* or *transition* (which have a similar meaning to 'bridge').

Rehearsal marks

Where there's a change in section, you'll often see a letter, usually in a square box, above the stave. Such markings are called *rehearsal marks* (or *section markings*) because they are useful when rehearsing – a band member or conductor may suggest 'let's take it from H', for example.

Measure numbers

A number placed above a bar line – on its own, in a circle or in a box – usually indicates the number of the following measure, counting from the beginning of the piece. Occasionally, however, numbers are used as rehearsal marks instead of letters.

Names, letters and numbers are used to identify the various parts of a piece

Section lines

Section lines – bar lines made up of two thin lines – are also sometimes used to indicate a change of section, as in the above example. They are also often used if there is a change of key signature.

Double bar line

The double bar line, consisting of a normal bar line and a thick bar line, is placed at the end of a piece. It is also used in repeat signs, which are explained in the next section.

The double bar line marks the end of a piece

REPEAT SIGNS

There are various signs and markings that tell you to repeat a measure, a section or even a whole piece of music.

One and two measures

The repeat sign for a single measure, a slash with a dot on each side, is commonly used. And sometimes the same symbol but with two slashes is placed on the bar line to indicate a repeat of two measures, as shown below.

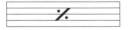

Repeat the previous measure

Repeat the previous two measures

Repeat from the beginning

If you come across a double bar line with two dots facing to the left, then you go back to the beginning of the piece and repeat everything you've played so far.

Repeat from the beginning

Two repeat signs

If there are two repeat signs with dots facing each other, you have to repeat the measures between these signs.

Repeat the measures between the two signs

Different endings

Sometimes a repeated section ends differently the second time around – this is indicated with square brackets marked 1 and 2, like in the example below. In this situation, you end the section the first time around with the measure marked 1, but when you get to this point again after repeating, you skip that measure and go straight to the measure marked 2. The terminology is self-explanatory: *first-time ending* and *second-time ending*.

You play this the first time but you skip it the second time

You play this the second time

Repeat the section between the repeat signs, but the second time miss out the measure marked 1, and go to the measure marked 2.

More than once

You may sometimes come across situations similar to the one described above, except that you need to repeat the section more than once. If, for example, you are required to play a section three times with the first ending and then use the second ending on the fourth time, you'd see '1, 2, 3' over the first bracket, and '4' over the second bracket.

SKIPPING AROUND

There are a variety of markings to indicate that you have to skip from one part of a piece to another.

- *Da Capo* (*D.C.*) When you reach a D.C. you return to the beginning of the piece and repeat. When you reach the D.C. the second time you ignore it, and go straight on.
- *Dal Segno* (*D.S.*) Segno is the Italian for sign. When you reach a Dal Segno or D.S., you go back to the 𝄋 sign. When you return to the D.S. again, you ignore it.

Coda

A *coda* (literally 'tail') is a section at the end of a piece of music. The sign ⊕ is used in conjunction with repeat instructions, and tells you to skip to the coda. You ignore the coda symbol until you have been instructed otherwise. A common example of such an instruction is *Da Capo al Coda* (or *D.C. al Coda*). When you reach this marking, you repeat from the beginning but when you get to the ⊕ you skip to the coda. Sometimes *Al* ⊕ is written instead of *Al Coda*.

Other coda markings

Coda markings can also be combined with other instructions. *Dal Segno al* ⊕, for example, tells you to go back to the 𝄋 symbol, continue to the ⊕, and then skip to the coda.

Fine

Al Fine means 'to the end'. *Da Capo al Fine* (or *D.C. al Fine*) is quite a commonly used marking; it means to go back to the beginning, and then finish the piece where you see the word *Fine*.

TAKE THE 'A' TRAIN

The melody of the jazz tune *Take the 'A' Train*, which was written by Billy Strayhorn and made famous by Duke Ellington, is printed on the next page. It's full of section signs and repeat marks, so provides a good example of many of the instructions introduced in this chapter.

The route

- Play part A twice – once with the first-time ending, the second time skipping the first-time ending and playing the second-time ending.
- Continue with part B.
- At the D.C. al Coda marking, go back to the beginning.
- Play section A until the coda symbol in measure 7.
- From the coda symbol, skip to the coda. These are the last two measures of the piece.

♩ = 120

Take the 'A' Train

Billy Strayhorn
Arr. B. Noorman

Take the 'A' Train, arranged by Bart Noorman

Words & Music by Billy Strayhorn © Copyright 1941 Tempo Music Incorporated, USA.
Used by permission of Cherry Lane Music Company.
All Rights Reserved. International Copyright Secured.

AABA

Although this may seem quite complicated, really the *form* of this piece is simply AABA – you play the A section twice, then the B section (the bridge), and finally A again. This simple form is used in lots of songs and jazz tunes – it just looks more complicated here because the A is a little bit different each time.

REPEATING NOTES AND CHORDS

There are also signs that tell you to repeat single chords and notes, and pairs of alternating notes.

Repeating chords

If a chord is followed by a slash or series of slashes, then you should repeat the chord once for each slash.

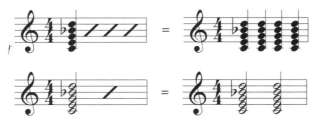

The slash sign tells you to repeat a chord

Repeating notes

A single note tells you how long to play for, and the slashes through the stem tell you what sort of notes to play. Here are some examples:

Alternating between notes

You may sometimes see two notes of different pitch indicated in a similar way. Again, the symbols are quite self-explanatory.

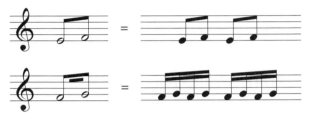

11. SCALES AND KEYS

It's possible to read music without knowing about scales and keys, but it's impossible to have any real understanding of what you're playing. And as well as helping you to understand why music works the way it does, knowing about scales and keys makes reading, improvising and writing your own music much easier.

Chapters 3 and 5 introduced the fact that an octave consists of twelve different notes. Few pieces of music, though, use all twelve of these notes, and most simple pieces use only seven or less. The notes used in a simple piece of music, arranged into order from lowest to highest (or vice versa) are the *scale* of the piece.

Major and minor

In Western music two types of scale – called *major* and *minor* – are much more significant than all the others. This chapter explains major and minor scales, and the *keys* that are based on them.

The tonic

Every piece of music has what is called a *tonic* – a note which is more important than all the others. A tune often starts on the tonic, and almost always finishes on it. Other names for the tonic are *keynote* and *home note*. The tonic of a piece is the first note of its scale.

Bah Bah Black Sheep

Bah Bah Black Sheep is written out overleaf. Try to play the tune, and feel how the opening C feels very strong. More importantly, feel how the second half of the tune feels like it's 'coming home' to the final C. If you stop on the D of 'three bags', the tune feels like it's been suddenly cut off and needs to fall back to the C to finish properly. This is because C is the tonic of the piece.

In order

If we arrange the notes of *Bah Bah Black Sheep* in order from lowest to highest, with the tonic (the C) at the bottom, we get the scale of the piece.

The scale of *Bah Bah Black Sheep*

Different situations

In this example the tune included all of the notes of the scale – you can tell because they occupy every line and space on the stave from the tonic upwards for a whole octave (from C to C). And in this example, the tonic happened to be the lowest note of the melody. However, some tunes don't include all of the notes of their scales, and the tonic isn't always the lowest note.

Tones and half-tones

The following diagram shows all the steps of the scale of *Bah Bah Black Sheep* on a piano keyboard. The step from C to D is a tone – you can tell because you have to miss out one note between them (C♯/D♭). The step from D to E is also a tone (missing out D♯/E♭). From E to F, however, is a half-tone, because you don't miss out a note between them.

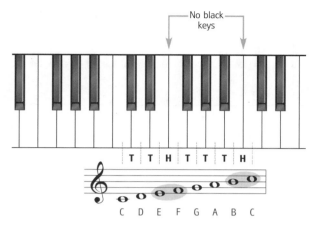

The scale of *Bah Bah Black Sheep*: all the steps are tones (T) except E–F and B–C, which are half-tones (H).

The major scale

The scale above consists of seven steps, five tones and two half-tones in the following order: T, T, H, T, T, T, H. Any scale with this arrangement of tones and half-tones is called a *major scale*.

Scales and keys

Scales are named after their tonic note. The scale of *Bah Bah Black Sheep* is a major scale with the tonic C – so it's called the *C major scale*. A piece of music that is based on a major scale is said to be in the *key* of that scale. So *Bah Bah Black Sheep* is in the key of C major.

The minor scale

The other important type of scale in Western music is the minor scale. Just like the major scale, the minor scale is simply a particular arrangement of tones and half-tones.

A minor

You can hear a minor scale by playing the white notes of a keyboard from A to A – this is the scale of *A minor*. It has a different character than the major scale, sounding sadder and darker – indeed, minor scales are often used for music with a melancholy character. As you can see in the following diagram, the order of steps in the A minor scale is: T, H, T, T, H, T, T.

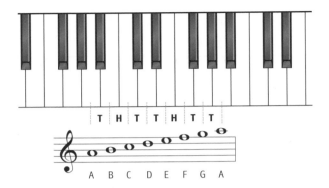

The minor scale, from A to A: T, H, T, T, H, T, T.

The natural minor

In some music various versions of the minor scale are used. This is explained in Chapter 14 – for now we'll just deal with the 'standard' minor scale as shown above, which is called the *natural minor scale*.

The same notes

You may have noticed that A minor and C major consist of the same notes, just with a different tonic. The diagram below shows how these notes can be arranged in a circle. The relationship between major and minor scales that use the same notes is explained in Chapter 14.

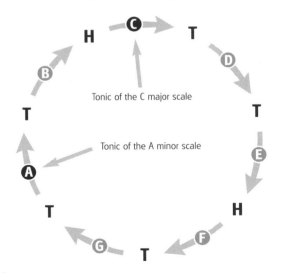

Tonic of the C major scale

Tonic of the A minor scale

MAJOR SCALES

The major scale can start on C, but also on any other note
– as long as the order of steps remains the same as it did in
C major: T, T, H, T, T, T, H.

From F to F

If you play the white keys from F to F, as shown below, the
order of tones and half-tones is T, T, T, H, T, T, H. This is
not the order of the major scale – there is a half-tone as the
fourth step instead of the third. You can hear the difference
if you play it.

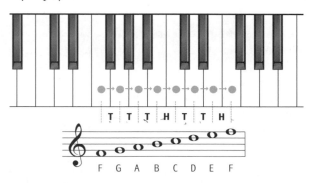

Correct the order

So if you want to play a major scale starting on F, you'll
have to change something to get the right order. The
solution is to lower the B by a half-tone by adding a flat.
The B then becomes a B♭. With a B♭, the order of tones and
half-tones is T, T, H, T, T, T, H – the correct order for the
major scale. So F to F with a B♭ instead of a B is the F
major scale:

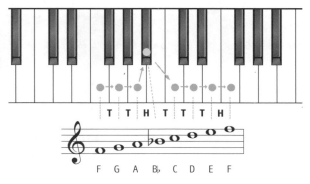

G major

F major needed a flat. But other scales need a sharp, or a number of sharps or flats. If you're trying to work out G major, for example, and you play the white notes from G to G, you'll find that the order of the last two steps differs from that of the major scale. The steps are T, T, H, T, T, H, T instead of T, T, H, T, T, T, H.

The natural notes from G to G: the order of the last two steps does not make a major scale.

Correct the order

Things go wrong when you step from E to F – this is a half-tone when it should be a tone. The solution is to raise the F by a half-tone, by turning it into F♯. Then the order will be correct – the scale of G major.

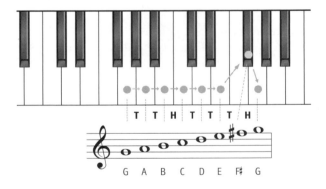

The scale of G major: the F is raised to F♯ to make the correct order of tones and half-tones.

Do, Re, Mi

Many people were taught Do–Re–Mi–Fa–So–La–Ti–Do at school. This is an example of a major scale. If you sing the first Do as an A, for example, the scale you'll be singing is A major. And if you start on an F♯, you'll be singing the scale of F sharp major.

Key signatures

In music written in G major, every F is raised to F♯. Instead of a sharp appearing in front of every F, a single sharp is written just after the clef on each stave – and this turns all the Fs in the whole piece into F♯s. This one sharp after the clef is the *key signature* of G major. Key signatures can have anything up to seven sharps or flats. To create the major scale of E flat major, for example, you need to lower three notes by a half-tone: B, E and A. So the key signature has three flats: B♭, E♭ and A♭.

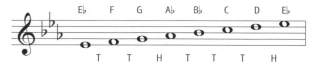

The scale of E flat major, with three flats

The major scales

The other major scales can be produced in exactly the same way. They're all in the following list, which shows which sharps or flats are in each key signature. If you want to see how these scales and key signatures look on the stave, turn to page 142.

key	tonic	number of sharps/flats in key signature	
C major	C	**0**	No sharps, no flats
G major	G	**1** ♯	F♯
D major	D	**2** ♯♯	F♯, C♯
A major	A	**3** ♯♯ ♯	F♯, C♯, G♯
E major	E	**4** ♯♯ ♯♯	F♯, C♯, G♯, D♯
B major	B	**5** ♯♯ ♯♯ ♯	F♯, C♯, G♯, D♯, A♯
F sharp major	F♯	**6** ♯♯ ♯♯ ♯♯	F♯, C♯, G♯, D♯, A♯, E♯
G flat major	G♭	**6** ♭♭ ♭♭ ♭♭	B♭, E♭, A♭, D♭, G♭, C♭
D flat major	D♭	**5** ♭♭ ♭♭ ♭	B♭, E♭, A♭, D♭, G♭
A flat major	A♭	**4** ♭♭ ♭♭	B♭, E♭, A♭, D♭
E flat major	E♭	**3** ♭♭ ♭	B♭, E♭, A♭
B flat major	B♭	**2** ♭♭	B♭, E♭
F major	F	**1** ♭	B♭

The major scales. The scales of F sharp major and G flat major sound the same – they are enharmonic (see page 76).

The same order

As you can see in the list, the sharps and flats always appear in the same order. With sharps, F♯ is always the first sharp to appear in any key signature, C♯ is the next, and then G♯, and so on. With flats, B♭ is first to appear, then E♭, then A♭, and so on.

The number

Once you're used to the various key signatures, you don't actually need to look at each individual sharp or flat sign and see which note it relates to. They appear in the same order, so if you see a key signature with two sharps, for example, you'll know that you have to raise every F and C to F♯ and C♯, because these are always the first sharps to appear. Likewise, if you see a key signature with one flat, you know that you have to lower every B to B♭.

Not so difficult

A piece with four or five sharps or flats looks a lot more complicated than it really is; you will soon learn exactly which notes the flats or sharps apply to. And once you've grasped the system underlying the order of the sharps and flats, it all becomes even easier. This system is dealt with in the next chapter.

Different keys

If the order of the tones and half-tones is the same in every major scale then why isn't everything just written in C major? Wouldn't playing be easier without all those sharps and flats? Yes, it would. But it would also make things pretty monotonous (which happens to mean 'one tone'). A piece in F major not only sounds at a different pitch from the same piece in C major, but it also sounds a little different. This is because different keys, like different colors, have their own character (although this is hard to hear). Also, it's easier to play certain keys, other than C major, on certain instruments.

MINOR SCALES

Obviously, there are just as many minor scales as there are major scales – you can start a minor scale on any note. Here are a few examples, before they are all listed.

From A to A: A minor

As we saw before, the minor scale is formed by the following order of tones (T) and half-tones (H): T, H, T, T, H, T, T. The A minor scale is found on the white notes between one A and the next A.

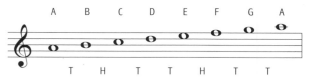

The scale of A minor

C minor

In order to stick to the same order when starting on C, you have to lower three natural notes: B to B♭, E to E♭ and A to A♭. So the scale of C minor has these three flats in its key signature.

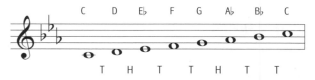

C minor: with a key signature of three flats

The lowered third note

If you play a major scale followed immediately by a minor scale with the same tonic (such as C major and C minor), you will hear a big difference at the third note. In C major the third note is an E; in C minor the third note is E♭. The difference in character between major and minor scales is mainly due to this third note. You can hear this difference even more clearly if you play a chord of C–E–G (a C major chord) and then a chord of C–E♭–G (a C minor chord). Chords are discussed further on page 111–112.

The minor scales

The following list shows all of the natural minor scales and their key signatures. Notice that the sharps and flats appear in exactly the same order as they do in the major scales. If you want to see these scales on staves turn to page 142.

key	tonic	number of sharps/flats in key signature	
A minor	A	**0**	No sharps, no flats
E minor	E	**1** ♯	F♯
B minor	B	**2** ♯♯	F♯, C♯
F sharp minor	F♯	**3** ♯♯ ♯	F♯, C♯, G♯
C sharp minor	C♯	**4** ♯♯ ♯♯	F♯, C♯, G♯, D♯
G sharp minor	D♯	**5** ♯♯ ♯♯ ♯	F♯, C♯, G♯, D♯, A♯
D sharp minor	E♯	**6** ♯♯ ♯♯ ♯♯	F♯, C♯, G♯, D♯, A♯, E♯
E flat minor	E♭	**6** ♭♭ ♭♭ ♭♭	B♭, E♭, A♭, D♭, G♭, C♭
B flat minor	B♭	**5** ♭♭ ♭♭ ♭	B♭, E♭, A♭, D♭, G♭
F minor	F	**4** ♭♭ ♭♭	B♭, E♭, A♭, D♭
C minor	C	**3** ♭♭ ♭	B♭, E♭, A♭
G minor	G	**2** ♭♭	B♭, E♭
D minor	D	**1** ♭	B♭

The minor scales. The scales D sharp minor and E flat minor sound the same; they are enharmonic (see page 76).

OTHER NOTES

Most pieces are based on the notes of one particular scale – but that doesn't mean that every note in the whole piece is one of the notes of that scale. *Take the 'A' Train* on page 60 is a good example. This piece is in C major, a scale without sharps or flats. Even so, some notes are raised or lowered by accidentals, like the G♯ in measure three.

Modulating

In some pieces the music changes key, a process called *modulation*. Changing key is important to most classical music, as well as music from some other genres. A piece which modulates usually starts in one key (the one indicated by the key signature), goes to one or more other keys in the middle, and then returns to the first key. A piece of music that starts and finishes in D major is said to be 'in D major', even if it modulates to various other keys in between.

Changing key signature

If a piece modulates, the key signature doesn't usually change – any extra sharps, flats or natural signs are written as accidentals. Sometimes, however, you'll see a new key signature written on the stave, after a section line.

WRITING AND PLAYING

A great way to really get to know and understand scales is to write them out. What does the E major scale look like, for example? Take a sheet of manuscript paper, and draw all the natural notes from E to E. Jot down the steps of tones and half-tones under the notes, then correct the order by raising or lowering notes using sharps or flats.

Is it right?

Your ears will probably tell you whether you got the correct scale when you try playing it. If you're not sure, check your scale with the ones on pages 142 and 143.

Scale wheel

The scale wheel on page 141 is a useful little device that shows you which notes belong to which major and minor scales.

12. THE CIRCLE OF FIFTHS

There is a system behind the fixed order of the sharps and flats in key signatures. The circle of fifths is a neat bit of theory that demonstrates this system.

In the previous chapter, you saw that C major has no sharps or flats. G major has one sharp (F♯), D major has two (F♯, C♯), and A major three (F♯, C♯, G♯). And so on.

A fifth higher

If you start on C and count five notes up the C major scale you come to G. In musical terms this distance is called a *fifth* – G is said to be a fifth higher than C. And whilst C major has no sharps, the major scale starting on G has one sharp. Then count up a fifth from G in G major, and you come to D – and D major has two sharps. Count five notes up from D in D major and you get to A, and the major scale starting on A has three sharps.

d e f♯ g a b c♯ d
g a b c d e f♯ g
c d e f g a b c

The major scale that starts a fifth higher has one extra sharp

The raised seventh

Which particular sharp is added also follows a pattern. Every time another sharp is added, it applies to the *seventh note* or *seventh step* of the scale. So the one sharp of G major is F♯ – the seventh note of the scale. The extra sharp needed to make D major is C♯, which is the seventh note of the scale.

Flats: a fifth lower

Scales with one or more flats are related in a similar way. To find the tonic of the scale with one more flat, you simply count five notes (a fifth) downwards. For example, C major has no flats. Count a fifth down from C in C major and you get to F – and the scale of F major has one flat. Count a fifth down from F in F major, and you get to B♭ – and B flat major has two flats.

c d e f g a b c
f g a b♭ c d e f
b♭ c d e♭ f g a b♭

The major scale that starts a fifth lower has one extra flat

The lowered fourth note

Every time a flat is added, it alters the fourth note of the new scale. B♭ is the fourth note of F major, E♭ is the fourth note of B flat major, and so on.

THE CIRCLE

The *circle of fifths* is a useful bit of theory, which shows all the major scales arranged in a circle. If you start at C and

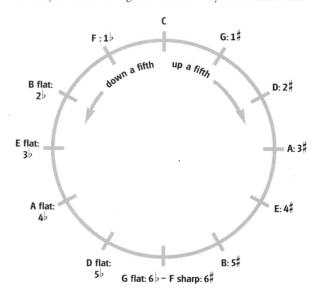

The circle of fifths showing the major scales

go round clockwise, you will see that a sharp is added each time. If you go around anti-clockwise, a flat is added each time.

Like a clock
Just like a clock, the circle of fifths is divided into twelve. There are five minutes between the numbers on the face of a clock. Similarly, there is always a distance of five steps (a fifth) between the scales adjacent on the circle.

The bottom of the circle
At the bottom of the circle, the sharps and the flats meet up: the G flat major scale with six flats and the F sharp major scale with six sharps appear at the same point. These two scales (and music based on them) look different on paper but sound the same. In the same way that G♭ and F♯ are enharmonic notes (see page 32), G flat major and F sharp major are *enharmonic scales.*

Other enharmonic scales
There are more enharmonic scales: C flat major (seven flats) sounds the same as B major (five sharps), and C sharp major (seven sharps) sounds the same as D flat major (five flats). This explains why very few pieces are written in key signatures with seven sharps or flats – you can always do with six or fewer.

The minor scales
The circle of fifths can also incorporate the minor scales. The complete circle, with the major and minor scales, is shown in Chapter 14 (page 92). That chapter also explains how major and minor scales relate to each other.

13. INTERVALS

Previous chapters have introduced the octave and the fifth as names for 'musical distances' from one note to another. The technical name for these distances is intervals, and a knowledge of intervals is essential if you want to really understand music.

Try playing a C and a G together, then play a C and a Db together. The first combination sounds quite pure, almost as if there was only one note, whilst the second combination is harsh on the ear. This is because the interval between C and G is different from the interval between C and Db, and each interval has its own character.

Second, third, fourth, etc

As was explained in the last chapter, the interval from C to G is called a fifth, because G is the fifth note, or *degree*, of the C major scale. The same logic applies to all the intervals formed between the tonic of a major scale and the other notes in the scale. D is the second note in the C major scale, for example, so the interval C–D is a called a *second*; A is the sixth note in the C major scale, so the interval C–A is called a *sixth*.

Unison and octave

If two notes are played or sung at the same pitch, there's no actual interval between the notes. This 'non-interval' is described by the word *unison*, which literally means 'one sound'. The octave is the eighth step in a major scale – such as from C to the next C in C major. This term comes from the Latin word *octo*, meaning eight.

On the stave

On a stave, the intervals between C and the other notes in C major look like this:

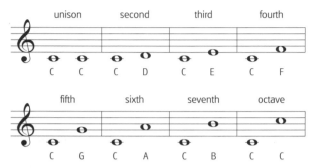

The intervals between C and the other notes of C major

PERFECT AND MAJOR

The distance from C to G is a fifth. From C to A is a sixth. But what about C to G♯, which is between G and A? To be able to name intervals such as this, a bit more knowledge is required.

Perfect and major

We've already seen the eight basic intervals of the major scale. These intervals can be divided into *perfect intervals* and *major intervals*. In all the following examples, the scale of C major is used.

Perfect intervals

Four intervals are called perfect, because they have an almost 'perfect', 'pure' sound when played as a chord: the unison (C–C), the fourth (C–F), the fifth (C–G), and the octave (C–C). When you play a two-note chord of one of these intervals, the notes seem to fuse together.

Major intervals

The other four intervals formed between the tonic of a major scale and the other notes in the scale are classed as *major intervals*: the *major second* (C–D), the *major third* (C–E), the *major sixth* (C–A), and the *major seventh* (C–B). If you play them, you'll hear that they do sound noticeably different from the perfect intervals. The second and the seventh clearly are much less 'perfect', while the third and the sixth sound somewhere in between.

The same in every scale

From the tonic up, every major scale is made up of the same series of perfect and major intervals. In the following diagram you can see how the intervals of C major are the same as those of E flat major.

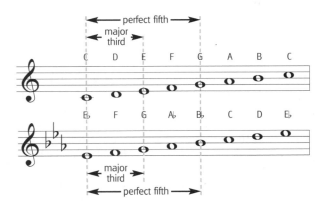

The intervals from the tonic to the other notes are the same in every major scale

MINOR, DIMINISHED AND AUGMENTED

If you reduce or enlarge an interval by a half-tone, its name changes, gaining one of the following words: diminished, minor or augmented.

Perfect, diminished and augmented

If you reduce a perfect interval by a half-tone it becomes diminished. For example, C–G is a fifth, and C–G♭ is a diminished fifth.

If you enlarge a perfect interval by a half-tone it becomes augmented. For example, C–G is a fifth, C–G♯ is an augmented fifth.

dimished ←— *reduce* —— **perfect** —— *enlarge* —→ **augmented**

Major, minor and augmented

If you reduce a major interval by a half-tone it becomes

minor. For example, C–A is a sixth, and C–A♭ is a minor sixth.

If you enlarge a major interval by a half-tone it becomes augmented. For example, C–A is a sixth, C–A♯ is an augmented sixth.

minor ◄———— reduce ———— **major** ——— enlarge ————► **augmented**

Diminished

A minor interval can be made smaller by another half-tone; it then becomes a diminished interval.

Up and down

The vertical order of the notes that make up an interval is important: a C and an E form a major third if the C is on the bottom (C–E), but a minor sixth if the E is on the bottom (E–C). Notice that if two notes form a major interval, then when they're swapped around, they always form a minor interval, and vice versa. So although from the tonic up a major scale consists of perfect and major intervals (C–C, C–D, C–E, etc), the intervals formed from the other notes up to the tonic (C–C, D–C, E–C, etc) are all perfect or minor intervals.

IN AN OCTAVE

On the following page you can see the intervals formed from C up to the octave. The perfect and major intervals are listed on the left of the keyboard diagram, the minor and diminished intervals to the right of the keyboard, and the augmented intervals on the far right.

Same sound, different name

Chapter 5 explained how two enharmonic notes sound the same and are played on the same notes, such as C♯ and D♭. Intervals work in exactly the same way – C–G♯ and C–A♭, for example, sound the same and are played on the same notes, yet C–G♯ is an augmented fifth, and C–A♭ is a minor sixth. These are called enharmonic intervals. Some enharmonic versions of intervals are not shown in the following keyboard diagram, such as the augmented unison (C–C♯), which sounds the same as a minor second (C–D♭). However, all the common names are shown.

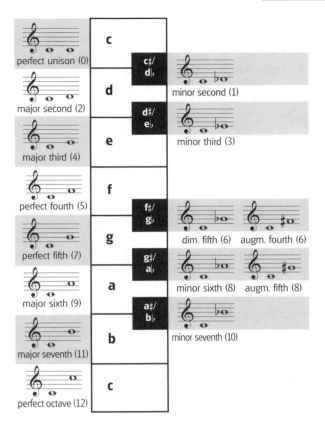

Intervals from C. The number of half-tones of each interval is given in brackets.

The tritone

The augmented fourth can also be referred to as the *tritone*, because it can be formed by three whole tones (such as C–D, D–E, E–F♯).

Bigger intervals

All the intervals introduced so far have been within the space of one octave. Bigger intervals work in exactly the same way – you just keep counting. From C to the D of the next octave is a *major ninth*, or to the E of the next octave is a *major tenth*. However, people rarely describe intervals bigger than two octaves in this way; you won't hear a musician talking about a 'twenty-fifth', for example.

Other scales

The examples in this chapter are all of the C major scale, starting from the tonic C. Naturally, the names of the intervals are exactly the same for all the other scales. C–E♭ is a minor third, and so is F–A♭ (A is the third step of the F major scale, so F–A is a major third, so F–A♭ is a minor third).

Not simply white notes

When trying to work out an interval between one note and another, it's important to count the steps of the scale starting on the bottom note – not simply the white notes. For example, at first glance the interval F–B may look like a perfect fifth, because there are five white notes from F to B. However, you need to count the steps from F in F major, and F major includes a B flat. So F–B♭ is a perfect fourth, and F–B is an augmented fourth. If you're not sure, you can always try counting the number of half-tones. A perfect fourth, for example, always consists of five half-tones. The number of half-tones in the various intervals are shown in brackets on the keyboard diagram on the previous page.

CONSONANT AND DISSONANT

Intervals can also be classified as either dissonant or consonant. *Dissonant* literally means 'not sounding together'. The notes in a dissonant interval seem to *dis*agree. They're not out of tune with each other, and their combined sound is not inherently ugly, but it feels as if there is tension between them.

Dissonant

The dissonant intervals are the major and minor seconds, the major and minor sevenths, the augmented fourth and the diminished fifth. There's no need to learn these by heart right away, but if you play them all, the reason for their common name should be clear.

Consonant

Consonant is the opposite of dissonant. The notes in a consonant interval seem to blend into each other. They sound purer, and less harsh on the ear.

Perfect and imperfect

The consonant intervals can be subdivided once more, into *perfect consonant* and *imperfect consonant* intervals. The imperfect intervals sound a bit less pure than the perfect ones.

- Perfect consonant intervals, as was explained earlier, are the unison, fourth, fifth and octave.
- Imperfect consonant intervals are the major and minor thirds, and the major and minor sixths.

Tension and resolution

Most genres of Western music make great use of the difference between dissonant and consonant intervals, especially the way that dissonant intervals create a kind of tension that can be *resolved* by consonant intervals. For example, feel the tension created when you play a chord of the notes C–F♯ (an augmented fourth) and then feel the resolution that is provided by following that chord with a chord of B–G (a minor sixth).

INTERVAL RECOGNITION

Being able to recognize intervals by ear, and to 'hear' them in your head without an instrument, is very useful – it will help you to be able to sing or imagine chords and melodies that are written down. Also, it makes it much easier to write and transcribe music.

Practicing intervals

There are lots of ways to develop your ability to recognize intervals. Just figuring out tunes on an instrument without the music helps. Or even better, have someone play two notes for you and see if you can recognize the interval – give it a while, as it's difficult at first.

Aural training

Recognizing intervals is an essential part of a wider set of skills – collectively known as *aural skills* – that includes writing down rhythms, melodies and chords that are played to you. There are many books, tapes, CDs and computer programs available for furthering your skill in this area. You'll find them in music stores labeled *aural training*, *ear training*, or *solfège*.

Well-known tunes

The easiest way to remember the sound of an interval is to know a tune beginning with that interval. Here are some examples. If you don't recognize the title of a particular tune, play it anyway – you may well find you know it.

Minor Second *Symphony no. 40* (W.A. Mozart)

Major second: *Frère Jacques, Frère Jacques*

Minor third: *Greensleeves*

Major third: *Oh, When The Saints*

Perfect fourth: *Amazing Grace*

Augmented fourth: Maria (Westside Story) (Leonard Bernstein)

Perfect fifth: *Twinkle Twinkle Little Star*

Minor Sixth: *Theme from Love Story* (Francis Lai)
Theme from the Paramount Picture LOVE STORY. Music by Francis Lai. © 1970, 1971 (Renewed 1998, 1999) by Famous Music Corporation. International Copyright Secured. All Rights Reserved.

Major sixth: *My Bonnie*

Minor seventh: Somewhere (Leonard Bernstein)
© Copyright 1956, 1957, 1958, 1959 by The Estate of Leonard Bernstein and Stephen Sondheim. Copyright Renewed. Leonard Bernstein Music Publishing Company Llc, Publisher. Boosey & Hawkes, Inc., Sole Agent. International Copyright Secured. Reproduced by permission of Boosey & Hawkes Music Publishers Ltd.

Major Seventh *I Love You* (Carl Porter)
© 1943 Chappell & Co, USA. Warner/Chappell Music Ltd, London W6 8BS. Reproduced by permission of International Music Publications Ltd.

Octave: *Somewhere Over The Rainbow* (Harold Arlen)
Words by E Y Harburg. © 1938 EMI Catalogue Partnership, EMI Feist Catalog Inc and EMI United Partnership Ltd, USA. Worldwide print rights controlled by Warner Bros Publications Inc/IMP Ltd. Reproduced by permission of International Music Publications Ltd.

14. MORE ABOUT MAJOR AND MINOR

This chapter looks in more depth at major and minor, introducing variations on the minor scale and relative keys, and providing tips on recognizing key signatures. All this will be useful whether you want to play or transcribe music, or simply understand it better.

Major and minor are the two most significant scales in Western music. And they each have various names.

Major
Generally, when describing a key or a chord, a letter on its own implies the major. For example, a tune 'in G' is a tune in G major, and a 'D chord' is a D major chord (chords are discussed in Chapter 18). For the sake of clarity, though, you will often see the word major, or the abbreviation *maj,* written after the letter. In classical music you may also come across the German word for major: *dur.*

Minor
Usually a minor key or chord is specified by simply putting the word minor, or the abbreviations *min* or *m,* after the letter, such as F minor, Fmin or Fm. Other ways to indicate the minor are with a minus sign (F-), a lower-case letter (f), or, in classical music, the German term: *moll.*

Church modes
Major and minor both originated as *church modes*, a series of scales from the Middle Ages. Their original names were *Ionian* (major) and *Aeolian* (minor). Church modes are explained in more depth in Chapter 15.

Major	Minor
Upper case (C)	Lower case (c)
maj	min, m, -
Dur	Moll (German)
Ionian	Aeolian

A variety of names for major and minor

Major third, minor third

The most important difference between major and minor is the interval between the tonic and the third step of the scale. In a major scale, this is a major third (such as C–E), whilst in a minor scale it's a minor third (such as C–E♭). Try playing a chord of the notes C and E, and hear how much brighter in character it sounds than the more melancholy combination of C and E♭.

THE SEVENTH

Another important difference between major and minor scales is the seventh step. Whilst a major scale has a half-tone from the seventh step to the tonic (B–C in C major, for example), a minor scale has a whole tone (B♭–C in C minor).

A strong pull

In major keys, because the interval from the seventh step to the tonic is a half-tone, the seventh step naturally leads to the tonic. Try playing the following example, and feel the 'pull' from the B to the C.

The B leads to the C

The leading note

Because of the way it 'leads' to the tonic, the seventh step in the major scale is called the *leading note*. Every major scale includes a leading note, because the seventh step is always one half-tone from the tonic: in D major, for example, the leading note is C♯, and in B♭ major the leading note is A.

Minor scales
The natural minor scale lacks a leading note, as the distance between the seventh step and the tonic is a whole tone. This means that it can't provide the powerful movement from the seventh step to tonic that the major scale does.

Classical music
In classical music the leading note is very important. In fact, it's so important that composers usually change the minor scale as they use it to create a leading note where appropriate. The way they do this is explained shortly, in the section titled 'Harmonic and Melodic Minor'.

Rock and pop
Generally, in rock and pop music the leading note is much less important, so most tunes in these genres don't alter the minor scale to create a leading note. Also thousands of rock songs that seem to be in a major key actually have a flattened seventh, and therefore no leading note. This altered major scale with a flattened seventh is the same as another of the old church modes – the *Mixolydian mode* (see page 95).

Jazz
Jazz music uses a bewildering variety of scales including 'standard' major and minor as well as altered versions. In some styles of jazz, the minor scale is altered to create a leading note just like in classical music, but other styles are more similar to rock in this respect.

HARMONIC AND MELODIC MINOR
Below is an example of a tune in D minor – there is no leading note since the interval between C and D is a whole tone. On the following page, the same tune is written but with the C raised to C♯ to form a leading note. Try playing

D minor without a leading note

The same tune, now with a leading note

both and you'll feel how the C♯ in the second example gives an extra 'pull' towards the final D.

Melodic minor

In classical music, this pull towards the tonic is so important that whenever a melody rises in a minor key, the seventh step of the scale is sharpened to form a leading note. However, because the leading note always wants to rise to the tonic, it's obviously not suitable for descending melodies. So in classical music, and some other styles, the minor scale used for melodies is different when it's going up from when it's going down. This two-way scale is called the *melodic minor scale*.

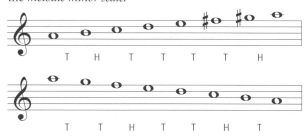

The A melodic minor scale – ascending and descending

The sixth step

You can see in the above example that in the rising version of the melodic minor scale the seventh step is not the only one that's raised by a half-tone – the sixth step is too (F to F♯ in this example). The reason is simple: if only the seventh was raised, there would be an interval of three half-tones between the sixth and seventh steps (F–G♯ in this case). This interval sounds very 'awkward' in a melody, and raising the sixth step gets rid of it.

Harmonic minor

The harmony (the chords) of a piece of music is based on a different version of the minor scale – the *harmonic minor*. Because chords don't ascend and descend in the same way as melodies, the harmonic minor scale is the same whether it's going up or down. When writing harmony, composers nearly always use a leading note, so the seventh step is raised in this scale. Unlike the melodic minor, the harmonic minor doesn't have a sharpened sixth step, because the interval of three half-tones that sounds awkward in a melody is not a problem in harmony.

The A harmonic minor scale – with an interval of three half-tones (3H) between the sixth and seventh steps.

Only variations

It's important to understand that the rising melodic minor scale and the harmonic minor scale are only alterations of the natural minor scale. You won't find a piece 'in G harmonic minor', for example. A piece 'in G minor' will make use of both G melodic minor and G harmonic minor.

Key signature plus accidentals

Because the harmonic and rising melodic minor scales are only variations of the natural minor scale, any sharp or natural symbols that they introduce are written as accidentals – put before the relevant notes rather than in the key signature. The example below is in D minor (using D melodic minor because it is a melody). The key signature is one flat, the key signature for any piece in D minor, and the B♮ and C♯ that come from the rising melodic minor scale are written as accidentals.

Tune in D minor using the rising melodic minor scale: the B♮ and C♯ are written as accidentals.

Leading tone and subtonic

The leading note is also known as the *leading tone*. Yet another name is the *subtonic* – literally 'under the tonic'.

RELATIVE MAJOR AND MINOR

In Chapter 11 all the major and minor key signatures were listed. You probably noticed that there were two scales – or keys – for each key signature. For example, there are two keys that have no sharps or flats (C major and A minor), two that have one flat (F major and D minor), and two that have one sharp (G major and E minor).

Relatives

Pairs of scales or keys that consist of the same notes are called relative scales or relative keys. A minor (A, B, C, D, E, F, G, A) is the relative of C major (C, D, E, F, G, A, B, C). The two scales use the same notes, but they have a different tonic.

Relative minors

Finding the relative minor of a major key is simply a matter of counting: the relative minor starts on the sixth step of the major scale. Two examples:

• The sixth step of F major (F, G, A, B♭, C, *D*, E, F) is D. So the relative minor of F major is D minor.
• The sixth step of G major (G, A, B, C, D, *E*, F♯, G) is E. So the relative minor of G major is E minor.

Relative major

Obviously, a similar rule works the other way around. The relative major of any minor key starts on the third step of the minor scale. Two examples:

• The *relative major* of A minor (A, B, *C*, D, E, F, G, A) is C major.
• The relative major of C minor (C, D, *E*♭, F, G, A♭, B♭, C) is E flat major.

Parallel keys

Don't get relative minors and majors (such as A minor and C major) confused with minor and major keys that share the same tonic (such as A minor and A major). Major and minor keys with the same tonic are known as *parallel keys*.

The circle of fifths

The minor keys can be fitted into the circle of fifths, each minor key paired with its relative major.

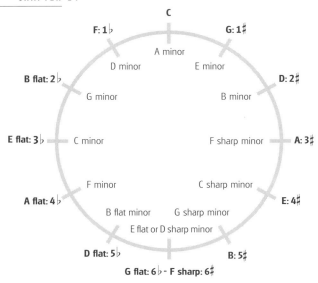

The circle of fifths showing relative major and minor keys

FIGURING OUT KEYS

It's useful to be able to figure out what key a piece is in, whether you're playing from sheet music, transcribing from a record, or playing a solo over a CD.

On paper

Working out the key of a piece that you have on paper is relatively simple. First, look at the key signature. With the technique shown below, you can immediately work out what pair of relative keys the signature implies.

Pointing sharps

If it's a key signature with sharps then look at the final sharp, and find the note one half-tone higher than that sharp. This will give you the root of the possible major key. In the example below there are four sharps. Look at the last sharp, in this case D♯, find the note one half-tone higher, in this case E. From that you can tell that the key is either E major, or its relative minor, C sharp minor.

The second-to-last flat

In flat key signatures, it's even easier. The second-to-last flat tells you the possible major key. In the example below, the second-to-last flat is a D♭, so the piece will either be in D flat major or in its relative minor, B flat minor.

The last sharp (D♯) points to the E. Therefore the key is E major, or its relative, C sharp minor.

The second-to-last flat is a D♭. Therefore the key is either D flat major, or its relative, B flat minor.

Which of the two

Once you know that the key is either the major or the minor of a pair of relatives, there are a few tricks to find out which one the piece is in. First, look at the last note of the melody and the bass line – in most cases, these notes will be the tonic of the key. Second, look for the leading note of the minor key. For example, if you're trying to work out whether you're in D major or B minor, and you see lots of A♯s, you're probably in B minor. If you're still not sure, try playing a couple of measures and you may well, especially after some practice, be able to just tell whether it's major or minor.

By ear

Figuring out the key of a piece of music by ear, from CD for example, is a bit more difficult, but it's not that hard after a bit of practice. First you need to find the tonic of the key. Go to the end of the track and try and listen to the last note in the melody and bass line – usually these are the tonic. Use an instrument to find out what note it is.

Then find the key

Once you have the tonic, try both the major and minor scales that begin on that note (they're all written out on pages 142 and 143). In most cases, you'll be able to hear which of the two scales best matches the music. This will (usually) be the key.

15. OTHER SCALES

Major and minor are the two most important scales in Western music, but they're not the only ones. This chapter looks at other scales – from those used in ancient church music to those used in the blues.

In Chapter 11, the C major and A minor scales were illustrated using a circle made up of tones and half-tones.

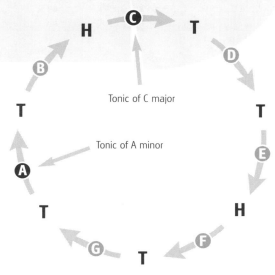

Playing from C to C gives you C major, and from A to A gives you A minor.

Other tonics

So, following the circle around from C to C gives a C major scale, whilst playing from A to A gives the A minor scale. These scales have different characters, even though they use the same notes, because the order of tones and half-tones is different. You can make more scales by starting on any of the other five notes and completing a circle, such as from D to D. Each resulting scale has a different character because, again, the order of half-tones and tones is different.

Church modes

In total seven scales can be generated from the circle on the previous page. These seven scales are called the *church modes*, as they were the basis of ancient church music. In the language of the church modes, the major scale is called the *Ionian mode*. The minor scale is the *Aeolian mode*. The other five scales also have their own names.

Ionian (major)	c d e f g a b c
Dorian	d e f g a b c d
Phrygian	e f g a b c d e
Lydian	f g a b c d e f
Mixolydian	g a b c d e f g
Aeolian (minor)	a b c d e f g a
Locrian	b c d e f g a b

Different characters

If you play around with these modes for a while, you'll start to get an idea of their characters. As mentioned in Chapter 14, many rock and pop songs are written in the Mixolydian mode, particularly rock 'n' roll and boogie-woogie tunes. The Phrygian mode is reminiscent of Spanish music, because Flamenco uses similar scales, whilst the Locrian mode sounds more jazzy.

Start on any note

Just like major and minor, each church mode is simply an arrangement of tones and half-tones, and therefore can be started on any note. The Dorian mode, for example, consists of the intervals T, H, T, T, T, H, T. The version of it that starts on D is only one of twelve possible versions. This version is called the D-Dorian, but if it started on C it would be called the C-Dorian.

Two extremes

The best way to hear the contrasting characters of two different modes is to play them one after each other starting on the same note. The Lydian and Locrian modes are written out below, both starting on C.

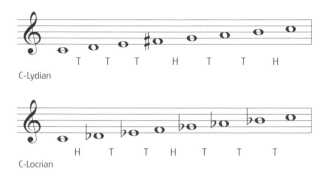

C-Lydian

C-Locrian

Modal music

The term *modal music* is sometimes used to describe music in which the character of the church modes is clearly identifiable. Usually there's not much harmonic activity in this type of music – you won't hear too many chord changes. In classical music, the church modes weren't used much after around 1600 until the twentieth century, when certain composers started using them again.

Modal jazz

It's not only classical music that can be modal. In the late 1950s, jazz trumpeter Miles Davis stopped relying on the fast chord changes that were essential in bebop (the main style of jazz from the previous years) and started writing what became known as *modal jazz*. His album *Kind of Blue* is perhaps the greatest example.

Diatonic scales

The seven church modes are also known as the *diatonic* scales. Each contains five whole tones and two half-tones, and is formed by two four-note halves, known as *tetrachords*. Ionian (major), Dorian and Phrygian scales have two identical halves – C-Ionian for example, is formed by the tetrachords C, D, E, F and G, A, B, C, each of which consists of the steps T, T, H.

NON-DIATONIC SCALES

This section introduces various non-diatonic scales – they have different arrangements of tones and half-tones, and some include steps of three half-tones. The following examples all start on C, making it easy to compare their characters, but, as with all the diatonic scales, they can each be started on any note.

Chromatic

The *chromatic* scale uses all twelve notes in the octave, so it consists entirely of half-tones. This scale is great for practicing: you play every note on your instrument if you keep going up or down as far as possible.

H   H   H   H   H   H   H   H   H   H   H   H

The chromatic scale

The whole-tone scale

As its name suggests, the *whole-tone scale* consists entirely of whole tones. It's also known as the *hexatonic* scale, because it's made up of six different notes (*hexa* = six).

T   T   T   T   T   T

The whole-tone scale

Octatonic

The *octatonic* scale is made up of alternating tones and half-tones, and consists of eight different notes (*octa* = eight). This scale is used a lot in jazz, and in the works of certain twentieth-century classical composers. There are two versions of this scale: one starting with a tone, the other starting with a half-tone.

H   T   H   T   H   T   H   T

The octatonic scale, starting with a half-tone

Pentatonic scales

Pentatonic scales consist of five different notes (*penta* = five). They are used in some pop, blues, and country and western, yet they can also have a strong Far Eastern flavor. The easiest way to hear a pentatonic scale is to play the black keys on a keyboard instrument. Try playing melodies as well as two-note chords (such as F♯–A♯, G♯–C♯, A♯–D♯).

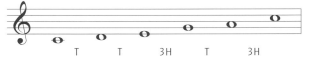

The pentatonic scale

Blues scales

Various scales are used in blues music, but the one shown below is extremely popular.

A well-known blues scale

The gypsy scale

The scale that is central to much folk music from Eastern Europe is often called the *gypsy scale*. Just like the blues scale above, this scale has an interval of three half-tones in two places.

The gypsy scale

16. TRANSPOSITION

Many wind and brass instruments are so-called trans-posing instruments, which means the notes they produce are different from the notes that are written down in their music. If you want to write for a transposing in-strument you need to know how to transpose – change music from one key to another.

When tenor sax players see a C on paper, in the third space of the treble clef, they close the key under their left middle finger – they *finger* a C. When they blow, though, the note that comes out is a B♭.

Concert pitch

The notes produced by non-transposing instruments are called concert pitch. So a C produced on the piano, a violin, or any other non-transposing instrument, is a 'concert pitch C'. The 'C' produced by a tenor sax is described as a 'concert pitch B♭'.

In B flat

The tenor sax is a *B flat instrument* – it is said to be *in B flat*, and have *B flat tuning*. Any B flat instrument produces a B♭ when reading and fingering a C. Other B flat instru-ments include the soprano saxophone, the B flat clarinet and the B flat trumpet.

In E flat

Any *E flat instrument* produces an E♭ when a C is read and fingered. Such instruments include both the alto and bari-tone sax, and the E flat clarinet.

Other keys

There are also instruments in various other keys. There are French horns, and alto and bass recorders in F, for example, clarinets in A, trumpets in D, and alto flutes in G.

Guitars and basses

Music for some instruments is written exactly an octave higher or lower than it sounds. Music for guitar, bass guitar and double bass, for example, is written an octave higher than it sounds, while music for the piccolo is written one octave lower. These instruments are *not* classified as transposing instruments.

The same fingerings

Different instruments of the same type – such as the various saxophones – all share the same fingering. No matter which type of sax a player is using, when they read a C, they press the same key. The same goes for any trumpet, any clarinet, and so on. However, if you gave four saxophone players (soprano, alto, tenor and baritone) the same piece of music displaying a middle C, they would each produce a different note, as shown below.

The notes produced when the four types of sax read a middle C

Octaves

As you can see from the above diagram, some transposing instruments transpose an octave more than their name suggests. The tenor sax is in B flat, for example, but when it reads a middle C the B♭ produced is not the one a tone below middle C, but the one an octave below that.

Every note changes

When a middle C is read by a soprano sax player, the note produced is the B♭ a whole tone lower than middle C. Obviously, it's not only middle C that changes: every other note the player reads will also sound a whole tone lower than what's written. When a G is read an F will sound, when a B♭ is read, an A♭ will sound. The same logic applies to all transposing instruments – when the alto sax reads a C it produces the E♭ a major sixth below middle C, so every note it reads will sound a major sixth lower.

Different music

The notes produced by a soprano sax are a whole tone *lower* than those written in the music. So when composers write a tune for a soprano saxophonist to play, they write out the music a whole tone *higher* than they actually want it to sound. This way the player just reads the music as normal and the resulting notes are the ones the composer wanted – as long as the player doesn't use any other type of sax to read a piece written for a soprano.

Changing the key

To take a piece and write it out higher or lower is a matter of taking it from one key and putting it into another. If you have a piece in C major, for example, and you want to rewrite it for the soprano saxophone, you have to move it up a tone. So you rewrite it in D major, because D is one tone higher than C. Changing the key of a piece is called *transposing*, and it isn't as hard as it may sound.

TRANSPOSING

Transposing is essential for dealing with transposing instruments, but also has other uses. For example, if a piece is too high or low in its current key for a particular singer or player you can simply transpose the music into a different key. Transposing sounds difficult, but it's actually very simple – and it's an excellent way to get used to scales, keys and intervals.

Two steps

The first thing to do is change the key signature to the new key. This automatically makes sure that all the intervals of the original will be maintained in the transposed version. Then you move all the notes to their new positions on the stave.

How it's done

In the following example, *Twinkle Twinkle Little Star* is transposed up a minor third from C major to E flat major.

Here's how it's done:
- Remember or check in this book for the key signature of E flat major – it has three flats.
- Take a piece of manuscript paper, and jot these three flats (B♭, E♭, A♭) next to the clef, in their proper position and order (see page 35).
- E♭ is a minor third higher than C. A third involves three steps, so move all the notes three places up the stave, including the original position as the first.

Twin - kle   twin - kle   lit – tle   star

Twinkle Twinkle transposed from up from C to E flat. The original notes are written in grey, the new notes in black.

Minor third, major third

Transposing up from C to E flat, *Twinkle Twinkle* went up a minor third. If you wanted to transpose the same tune from C to E (now a *major* third), the notes would be moved to the same positions on the stave as they were for E flat major, but the key signature would be different (it would have four sharps).

From E flat to B

Transposing a piece into any major key is just as easy as from C to E flat (and the same is true of transposing a minor piece into another minor key). This example shows the E flat major version of *Twinkle Twinkle* being transposed up into B major:
- The B major scale has five sharps. Write them down next to the clef.
- The interval from E♭ to B is an augmented fifth (E(♭), F, G, A, B).

Twin - kle   twin - kle   lit – tle   star

Twinkle Twinkle transposed from E flat to B. The three flats of E flat major have been replaced by the five sharps of B major. The original notes are grey, the new notes are black.

- So move the notes up five places, including the original position as the first.

Transposing accidentals

If a note has an accidental, things get a little bit more complicated – sometimes a sharp or flat sign needs to be turned into a natural sign or vice versa. All you need to do is work out which degree of the scale you're dealing with in the original, and make sure the same degree of the scale is represented in the new version.

The degree of the scale

In the following example, a melody is transposed from B flat major down a minor third to G major. The new key signature is put in place, and the notes are moved three places down the stave. The E♮ in the original, however, becomes a C♯, in order to make sure the same degree of the scale is represented in the new version. In the original, the accidental was raising an E♭ (the fourth degree of the B flat major scale) to an E♮. So in effect it was acting as a sharp, and the E♮ is the sharpened fourth degree of the scale. In G major, the sharpened fourth degree is C♯.

A tune transposed from B flat major to G major. The natural sign becomes a sharp.

17. OTHER METERS AND RHYTHMS

This chapter looks at strong beats and weak beats, irregular time signatures, and introduces the swing and the clave.

In a piece in $\frac{4}{4}$ you can usually hear quite easily where the first beat is – it sounds and feels a little stronger than the rest, which is why it's known as a *strong beat*. The third beat in each measure, though slightly less strong than the first, is also a strong beat. These strong beats are also referred to as *on-beats*, *metric accents*, and *accented beats*, while the second and fourth beats in each measure are known as the w*eak beats* or *off-beats*.

Rock, pop and jazz

In most rock and pop tunes, the drummer accents the weak second and fourth beats on the snare drum. Drummers call these beats *afterbeats* or *backbeats*. Jazz drummers often accent them by closing their hi-hat cymbals with the left foot. The first and third beats, however, still feel stronger – audiences tend to clap on 1 and 3, even when the drummer is accenting 2 and 4 on the snare drum.

Triple meter

Beats 1 and 3 are also the strong beats in a measure of triple meter, such as $\frac{3}{4}$. However, the effect is different as you get two strong beats next to each other – the third beat of one measure and the first beat of the next measure.

Downbeats and upbeats

The first beat of a measure is also called the *downbeat* (because a conductor usually indicates this point with a downward motion) and the *principal metric accent*. The last beat of the measure is often called the *upbeat*.

IRREGULAR METERS

Chapter 4 introduced duple, triple and quadruple time, but these are not the only types of meter. There is also *quintuple time*, which has five beats in a measure (such as $\frac{5}{4}$) and *septuple time*, which has seven beats in a measure (such as $\frac{7}{4}$). These are sometimes referred to as *irregular meters* or *odd time signatures*.

Different accents

A measure in an irregular meter is usually divided into two groups of beats, and the division defines the pattern of strong and weak beats. For example, a measure of five-four can be a group of three beats followed by a group of two (in which case the strong beats are 1 and 4), or a group of two beats followed by a group of three (with the strong beats 1 and 3).

Counting in groups

Irregular meters can be counted in these sub-groups. The example below is a tune in five-four, with each measure consisting of a group of three followed by a group of two – the strong beats are 1 and 4. This tune can be counted '1, 2, 3, 4, 5' as shown, or as '1, 2, 3, 1, 2' to emphasize the groups.

A tune in five-four. In this example the strong beats are 1 and 4.

Take Five

One of the few really well-known tunes in an irregular meter is the jazz standard *Take Five*, written by alto saxophonist Paul Desmond for pianist Dave Brubeck's group in the late 1950s. Like the example above, *Take Five* is in five-four, with each measure consisting of a group of three beats followed by a group of two.

CHAPTER 17

SWING

The word *swing* is used mostly in jazz. In swing style, eighth notes are played and felt like triplets rather than regular, 'straight' notes – they're played with a *triplet feel.*

Written as eighth notes

The parts that jazz players read from show normal eighth notes. To indicate that they're to be played with a triplet or swing feel, the music may have the word 'swing' written at the top, or a key as shown on the right.

Swing style: play the eighth notes as the first and last notes of a triplet

Straight eighths

Some pieces have sections that you play as swing and others where you have to play normal eighth notes. The terms that refer to normal eighth notes are *straight eighths, even eighths,* or *even 8ths.*

OTHER PATTERNS OF ACCENTS

In most pop, rock and classical music, the accented beats are governed by the time signature: there are one or more accents in each measure, usually on the first and third beat. Sometimes, though, especially in jazz, these accents are 'hidden', and other places, such as the eighth note after the first beat, are accented. This is called *syncopation.*

The clave

There's also music where the main accents make up a pattern that is spread over two or more measures. A lot of Latin American music, for example, is based on a rhythmic pattern called the *clave,* which has five accents over two measures. It may be played as shown below, which is called the 3-2 clave, or the other way around (starting on the second measure) in which case it's called the 2-3 clave.

The 3-2 clave: five accents spread out over two measures

Changing meters

In the examples in this book, the meter has always remained

constant throughout a piece. However, in some music, especially twentieth-century classical music and music with Arabic influences, the time signature can change every measure or two. And a composer can use an endless variety of irregular meters, such as $\frac{9}{16}$ (nine sixteenth notes in a measure) or $\frac{13}{8}$ (thirteen eighth notes in a measure). However, you're unlikely to come across such complicated time signatures in most styles of music.

Polyrhythm

Polyrhythm is when two or more rhythms of different length or with different accents or divisions are played simultaneously. A very simple example is when a pattern of eighth notes is played over a pattern of triplets, but some styles – mainly played in Africa – are hugely complicated, with many musicians each playing a pattern of different length and meter.

18. CHORDS, TAB AND DRUM MUSIC

The standard system of music notation, as explained in this book, allows for the writing down of music for most instruments. However, various other systems are also used – guitarists read chord charts and tablature, drum music has its own system, and jazz chords can be written as letters and numbers. All these system are explained in this chapter.

The guitar is one of the world's most popular instruments, largely because it can provide chords for people to sing along to. Chords are easy to play on the guitar, but when notated with staves and notes they are very difficult to read. So except in classical music, chords for guitarists are usually written in *chord charts*, or *chord diagrams*.

CHORD CHARTS

Chord charts are easy-to-read little diagrams that show you where to place your fingers to play a particular chord. Most rock and pop sheet music includes chord charts just above the vocal line. You'll find an example on the following page.

How they work

Your fingers are numbered from 1 to 4, from your index finger to your little finger. So, the following example tells you to play string 3 at the first fret with your index finger, string 5 at the second fret with your middle finger, and string 4 at the second fret with your ring finger. The result is an E major chord (see page 111).

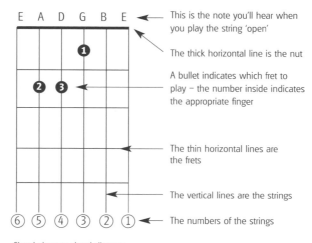

E A D G B E ← This is the note you'll hear when you play the string 'open'

The thick horizontal line is the nut

A bullet indicates which fret to play – the number inside indicates the appropriate finger

The thin horizontal lines are the frets

The vertical lines are the strings

⑥ ⑤ ④ ③ ② ① ← The numbers of the strings

Chord chart or chord diagram

TABLATURE

Tablature, or *tab*, is another system for writing down guitar and bass music – not just chords, but solos and melodic lines too. Most music stores have books of songs with the guitar parts written in tab. Tab doesn't allow for the indication of exact rhythm, so the music is usually written out on a normal stave above or below (if you know how the tune should sound, though, you'll know the rhythm, and so will only have to read the tab line). The tablature staff represents a guitar neck – here's how it works:

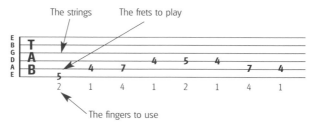

The strings   The frets to play

The fingers to use

The six horizontal lines represent the six strings of the guitar and the numbers on the lines tell you which frets to play. Bass tablature works the same way but there are only four lines. If there are also numbers underneath the lines, they tell you which finger you should use to fret each note. The above example is a boogie-woogie bass line.

Other instruments

Although the word tablature usually applies to guitar music, it also describes any system of writing down music that involves a diagram instead of notes. For example, flute tablature shows which keys to hold down to create a certain note, and piano tablature, as shown below, shows how to create a certain chord.

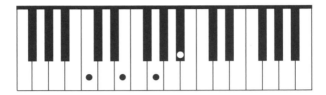

Keyboard tablature

DRUM MUSIC

Drum music is written on a regular five-line stave, but the notes, instead of indicating various pitches, represent different parts of the drum kit. However, every player uses a different set-up – one drummer may have ten cymbals and six toms, whilst another may have only two cymbals and two toms – so drum music cannot always indicate exactly which bit of the kit to play. Partly for this reason, drum notation isn't completely standardized.

Drums and cymbals

Generally, a drum is represented with a 'solid' note head, and a cymbal is written with a cross as a note head. Some drum music has a kind of key at the beginning, explaining exactly which kinds of drums and cymbals are represented by which notes. But even then, which particular crash cymbal or tom is to be played is left to the discretion of the drummer. Usually, the following notes are used for the core parts of the drum kit.

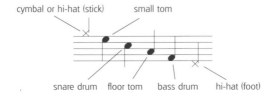

cymbal or hi-hat (stick)   small tom

snare drum floor tom bass drum hi-hat (foot)

On paper

You hardly ever see a drummer on stage with a music stand – and often the sheet music for a song doesn't include a drum part, simply having something like 'slow rock beat' written at the beginning. However, there's lots of written material available for drummers, ranging from exercises to solo pieces. Here's an example of how a simple rock rhythm looks.

A simple rock rhythm

BUILDING CHORDS

Especially in music for jazz pianists and guitarists, chords are often just written as a letter and a number. The letter refers to the *root* of the chord – the note it is based on and named after – and the number refers to the other notes in the chord. A full description of chord abbreviations is beyond the scope of this book, but this section explains the basics.

The third

The interval of a third is the building block of chords. Indeed, chords in Western music are based on 'piles' of thirds.

Triads

A *triad* is a chord of three notes. A C major triad (written simply as 'C') consists of the notes C–E–G, scale degrees 1–3–5 of C major. A G minor triad (written 'Gm' or 'Gmin') consists of G–B♭–D, scale degrees 1–3–5 of G minor. Chords can also be described in terms of the intervals between the notes: a major triad is a minor third on top of a major third, and a minor triad is a major third on top of a minor third.

The seventh

If you add a fourth note to a triad, you simply add another third on the pile. A third up from scale degree 5 is scale degree 7, so you add a seventh. However, there is a slight complication here: in chords, sevenths are always flattened unless otherwise stated. Chords with four or more notes are written simply as their root and highest note. So, a C^7 is C–E–G–B♭ (scale degrees 1–3–5–♭7 in C major). Only if the seventh is preceded by a 'major', or 'maj', is the seventh not flattened: so a Cmaj^7 chord is C–E–G–B.

Bigger chords

If you play jazz you'll come across many chords with bigger numbers, but the logic remains the same: build up the chord in thirds, including a flattened seventh, until you come to the number in question. For example, a C^{13} chord consists of C–E–G–B♭–D–F–A (scale degrees 1–3–5–♭7–9–11–13).

Missed out notes

Although the theory above shows that each chord is a stack of thirds, in some chords certain notes are usually left out. For example, a jazz musician will usually omit the third degree in an eleventh chord, and the eleventh degree in a thirteenth chord.

Sharps and flats

Each of the individual notes in a chord can be specified as a sharp or flat. A $C^{♯9}$ chord, for instance, consists of C–E–G–B♭–D–F♯. Often, though, when one note is altered, all the other notes from the seventh up are also included in the name for clarity – so a $C^{♯9}$ is often written as $C^{7♯9}$.

Other chords

In real terms, composers can, and do, use any combination of notes to form a chord, but these piles of thirds form the basis of the theory behind chords. Also, every chord can be *inverted* (with the notes in a different order), have any of their notes *doubled* (played at more than one octave), played without every one of their notes, or changed further with extra signs and symbols.

19. WRITING MUSIC DOWN

If you can read music, you can also write it down. This is useful whether you want to jot down an idea to return to later, notate music for band members, or compose an entire symphony. And writing music can also be good theory practice – there's no better way to learn scales, keys or chords than writing them out.

You can buy *manuscript paper*, music paper with pre-printed staves, in any music store. There are lots of types available, from standard A4 pads with 16 staves per sheet, and paper for particular instrumental combinations, to 64-stave orchestral paper. You'll find some blank staves on page 146 of this book – you can photocopy the page to produce manuscript paper.

Pens and pencils
Most musicians use a pencil to sketch out material. Quite soft ones, such as a 2B, are the best to use, as they're easy to rub out, and a propelling pencil saves you permanently having to use a sharpener. When you're copying up final versions, pencil is no good as it smudges easily. Either use a pen (fine-liners work well) or write a master very clearly with pencil and then photocopy it – this way you can always edit and re-photocopy your original later.

Note heads
Making perfectly even, round note heads is difficult and time-consuming with a pencil or pen. When writing ideas down, or sketching things for themselves to play, most composers draw solid note heads (quarter notes, etc) as

kind of diagonal lines. However, if you need someone else to be able to read what you've written, it's worth spending a little extra time on the note heads.

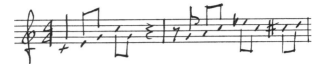

Note heads are often drawn as diagonal lines

Stems

When writing a single-voice melody, the notes above the third line are usually written with their stems pointing down (from the left side of the note head). Notes below the third line are written with their stems pointing up (from the right side of the note head). Notes *on* the third line (B in the treble clef, D in the bass clef) can point either way. Obviously, though, these are not strict rules as you often have to beam together a group of notes including some above and some below the third line. If you want to combine two melodies – such as two trumpet parts – on one stave, then write the lower one with all the stems going down and the other with all the stems going up.

Alignment

The term *alignment* refers to the way that the rhythms of different staves line up with each other – whether it's the left and right hand of a piano piece, or two different instrument parts in a score. It's important to write with good alignment, because if you don't your music will be very difficult to read. In a correctly aligned piece, notes or rests that are played at the same time line up exactly, as in the example below.

The rhythm of each part should be correctly aligned

A few tips

Here are a few more tips for writing legibly:

- Tails, or flags, are always drawn on the right of the stem.
- Draw accidentals on the same level and just before the notes they apply to.
- Writing a quarter rest is easy if you think of it as a tilted Z over a capital C.
- Reading is easier if every measure is roughly the same length, within reason. Avoid squashing measures up.
- Never split a measure over two lines. It's better to have a gap at the end of a stave than to have a split measure.
- You'll save a lot of time if you use shorthand techniques, such as the repeat signs for chords and measures (see Chapter 10).

Computers

Computers can also be used for notation. Given the right software and hardware, your computer can be an enormous help – you can transpose at the touch of a button, you can write a score and have the computer instantly print out the separate parts for each player. And with a MIDI keyboard hooked up to your computer, you can play music on the keyboard and have it appear on a stave on the screen. However, to make all this work very effectively with anything apart from very simple music, you need quite expensive equipment and time to learn how to use it.

20. BACK IN TIME

Western musical notation has evolved over more than a thousand years, changing over time to keep up with developments in music. This chapter takes a quick look at the history of notation – from neumes to notes, and from lines to staves.

The chromatic scale, dividing the octave into twelve equal steps, was created as long as 2,500 years ago by Pythagoras, the famous Greek philosopher and scientist. About a thousand years later these notes were given their letter names.

Written music

Some of the oldest surviving examples of written Western music are the Gregorian chants, named after Pope Gregory the Great (540–604). From the seventh century, a system evolved whereby little marks (neumes) were added to the texts of these chants, to indicate the direction of the melody.

Lines

By the middle of the eleventh century, it was common practice to scratch a single line in the paper to indicate a particular pitch. Soon after that a four-line staff came into being, which often had the lines drawn in different colours – an invention of the Italian monk Guido of Arezzo (c.995 –1050). Using this staff, singers could read all the notes of the Gregorian chants for the first time. Many of the modern-

A four-line staff with Gregorian music

day notes and rests can already be recognized in manuscripts dating from that time.

Ut, Re, Mi

Once the four-line staff had been introduced, Guido of Arezzo tackled the problem of how people could learn to read it. His solution was to use a hymn to Saint John as a guide – the first syllable of each line was paired with the note that it was sung on, resulting in the sequence Ut–Re–Mi–Fa–Sol–La.

The hymn to Saint John

Do, Re, Mi

Around 1600, a seventh note was added to the sequence, which then covered the entire major scale: Ut–Re–Mi–Fa–Sol–La–Si–Ut. The 'Si' was a combination of the first letters of Sancte Ioannes (Saint John). Later, Sol became So, Si became Ti, and the church changed the syllable Ut to Do, on the grounds that God (**Do**minum) was the beginning and the end of all things. This resulted in the Do–Re–Mi system, which is still taught in schools today.

The five-line stave

The five-line stave has been common since the thirteenth century, and apart from certain ornaments and symbols for new styles, musical notation has remained basically unchanged since the seventeenth century.

SIGNS AND MARKINGS

In the list below you'll find the signs and symbols covered in this book. The numbers in brackets refer to the pages where you can find more information on each symbol.

PITCH

𝄞	treble clef or G clef *(17)*
𝄢	bass clef or F clef *(17)*
𝄡	alto clef or C clef *(19)*
♯	sharp *(31)*
♭	flat *(31)*
𝄪	double sharp *(38)*
𝄫	double flat *(38)*
♮	natural *(34)*

RHYTHM

	bar line *(11)*
4/4	time signature *(11)*
C	common time *(12)*
¢	alla breve *(12)*
⌐3¬ bracket	triplet *(26)*
·	dot *(23)*
⌣	tie *(25)*
♩=120	metronome marking *(42)*

DYNAMICS

p	piano *(39)*
pp	pianissimo *(39)*
ppp	pianississimo *(39)*
mp	mezzo-piano *(39)*
mf	mezzo-forte *(39)*
f	forte *(39)*
ff	fortissimo *(39)*
fff	fortississimo *(39)*
sf sfz	sforzando *(41)*
fp	fortepiano *(41)*
<	crescendo *(40)*
>	decrescendo *(40)*

REPEAT AND SECTION

	repeat sign *(58)*
⁄.	repeat previous measure *(57)*
⁄⁄.	repeat previous 2 measures *(57)*
/	repeat previous chord *(61)*
𝄋	segno *(59)*
⊕	coda sign *(59)*
1⃒ 2⃒	first time ending *(58)*
	section line *(57)*
	double bar line *(57)*
C	rehearsal mark *(57)*
25	measure number *(57)*

ARTICULATION

⌢	phrase mark *(47)*
⌣	slur *(47)*
⌢	fermata *(48)*
>	accent *(46)*
∧	intense accent *(46)*
−	tenuto *(48)*
.	staccato *(47)*
▾	staccatissimo *(47)*
♩♩°	du-wah *(50)*
⌣	scoop *(49)*
♩×	ghost note *(50)*

ORNAMENTATION

tr	trill *(51)*
↭	mordent *(51)*
↭	inverted mordent *(52)*
trem.	tremolo *(52)*
♪	acciaccatura *(53)*
♪	appoggiatura *(53)*
∼	turn *(54)*
↗	glissando *(54)*
↘	fall *(55)*
↗	lift *(55)*
↘	plop *(55)*
♪	doit *(55)*

GLOSSARY AND INDEX

This glossary-index provides short definitions of all the terms and abbreviations mentioned in this book, and some others that you may occasionally come across. The numbers in brackets refer to the pages where the subject is dealt with in more detail.

8va *(20)* Play all marked notes an octave higher than written. If this marking (or *8va bassa* or *8va sotto*) is written below notes in the bass clef you should play all the notes an octave lower than written. A 15 instead of an 8 implies a change of two octaves. The term 'loco' instructs you to return to the written pitch.

15va See: *8va.*

A tempo *(44)* Return to the original tempo, after a quicker or a slower section. Also indicated as 'Tempo Iº' (pronounced 'tempo primo').

Accelerando, accel., acc. *(44)* Gradually speed up.

Accent *(46)* A note with an accent is emphasized, played with extra force. See also: *Natural accents.*

Accented beat *(104)* See: *Natural accents.*

Acciaccatura *(53)* A type of ornament, written as a small note with a slash through it. Also known as 'grace note'.

Accidentals *(36, 90)* Sharps, flats or natural signs that are not in the key signature. An accidental only applies to the note it is written before and to any notes of the same pitch that follow it in the same measure.

Ad libitum *(44)* Literally

119

'at liberty'. Often abbreviated to 'ad lib'.

Adagio *(43)* A slow tempo (metronome marking 66–76). See also: *Metronome marking.*

Aeolian mode *(95)* Another name for the minor scale. The Aeolian mode is the sixth church mode. See also: *Church modes* and *Minor scale.*

Afterbeat *(104)* Term used mainly in rock and pop music. The drummer often hits the snare drum on the afterbeats – usually the second and fourth beats in a four-four measure.

Agitato *(45)* Agitated.

Agogic accent See: *Tenuto.*

Al coda *(59)* Literally 'to the coda'. See also: *Coda.*

Al fine *(59)* 'To the end'. Often appears with the marking Da Capo. 'Da Capo al Fine' tells you to play from the beginning and finish at the word 'Fine'. See also: *Da Capo.*

Alla breve *(12)* Another name for the time signature with two half-note beats in a measure ($\frac{2}{2}$), which is also called 'cut common time' and indicated with the symbol ₵. Sometimes alla breve is written as an instruction in a piece in $\frac{4}{4}$, in which case you are meant to play with a 'half-note feel', as if the piece was in cut common time.

Allargando *(44)* Get slower, and perhaps also louder. Literally 'broadening'.

Allegro, Allegretto, Allegrissimo *(43)* Allegro is a quick, lively tempo (metronome marking 120–168). Allegretto is less fast, allegrissimo is a little faster. See also: *Metronome marking.*

Alto clef *(19)* A clef which sets middle C as the third line of the stave. It's also called the 'alto clef', and is most commonly used for viola music. See also: *Clef.*

Andante *(43)* A medium tempo (metronome marking 76–108), often described as walking pace. See also: *Metronome marking.*

Antimetric *(28)* 'Against the rhythm'. Triplets, septuplets and quintuplets are examples of antimetric figures.

Appoggiatura *(53)* A type

of ornament. A small note which is written before and takes up around half the time of a normal-sized note.

Arpeggio *(49)* A chord which is 'spread out', so that its notes are sounded one by one.

Articulation markings *(46–50)* Markings which indicate how notes should be played, such as staccato (shortened), legato (smoothly) and the accent (with emphasis).

Assai *(45)* Usually means 'extremely', but occasionally means 'sufficiently' or 'enough'. Used in combination with other indications.

Augmented *(79–82)* An augmented interval is a major or perfect interval enlarged by a half-tone. For example, C–F is a perfect fourth, so C–F♯ is an augmented fourth. See also: *Intervals.*

B flat instruments *(99)* Instruments which produce a concert pitch B♭ when a C is read and fingered. See also: *Transposing instruments.*

Bar See: *Measure.*

Bar lines *(11, 57)* The ver-

tical lines on the stave that mark where one measure ends and another begins. A bar line consisting of two thin lines is called a 'section line', and a bar line with one thick and one thin line – the 'double bar line' – is written at the end of a piece. See also: *Measure, Meter* and *Time signature.*

Bass clef *(17)* A clef which sets the fourth line of the stave as the F below middle C. Also called the 'F clef'. See also: *Clef.*

Beams *(8–10)* Beams are the lines that join eighth notes and shorter notes into groups (replacing their tails), making music easier to read. The groups usually add up to one beat, two beats, or half a beat.

Beats per minute, BPM *(42)* The number of beats per minute indicates the tempo of a piece. See also: *Metronome marking.*

Black notes The notes produced by pressing the black keys on a keyboard instrument are sometimes referred to as black notes. See also: *White notes.*

Blues scale *(98)* A scale used for playing blues music. The classic blues scale includes two intervals of three half-tones.

BPM See: *Beats per minute.*

Bridge *(56)* A section of a piece that 'bridges' two other sections.

C clef *(19)* Alternative name for the 'alto clef'. See: *Alto clef.*

Capo *(59)* The beginning of a piece. See: *Da Capo* and *Al Fine.*

Chart Another term for score, or part, especially used by jazz musicians.

Chord *(21, 61, 108–112)* Two or more notes sounded together.

Chord chart, chord diagram *(108–109)* Small diagram that represents the guitar fretboard, showing the player where to put the fingers to create a chord.

Chromatic scale *(97)* A scale made up entirely of half-tones, and therefore including every note used in Western music (C, C♯, D, D♯, E, etc).

Chromaticism The use of lots of chromatic notes (notes not in the key signature of the prevailing key).

Church modes *(95–96)* There are seven church modes or scales. They can all be played on the white notes on a keyboard: from C to C is the first (the *Ionian mode*), D to D is the second (the *Dorian mode*), and so on. See also: *Diatonic, Major scale* and *Minor scale.*

Circle of fifths *(74–76, 91–92)* In theory: a diagram that highlights how all major and minor keys are related in terms of the interval of a fifth. In practice: the use in a piece of a series of chords in the order found in the circle of fifths.

Clave *(106)* A two-measure rhythmic pattern central to much Latin American music.

Clef *(17–19)* A clef is a symbol that specifies the pitch of a particular line on a stave (and in turn the pitches of all the other lines and spaces). The 'treble clef' or 'G clef', for example, is an elaborate letter G on the second line, specifying this line as the note G above middle C. The other clefs still regularly used are the 'F clef' or 'bass clef', and the 'C clef' or 'alto clef'.

Coda *(59, 60)* Literally 'tail'. A closing section at the end of a piece.

Common time *(12)* Another name for four-four time ($\frac{4}{4}$). See also: *Four-four time, Time signature* and *Meter*.

Compound time, compound meter *(29–30)* Any time signature in which a dotted note is counted as the beat. In $\frac{6}{8}$, the most common example, every measure contains two dotted quarter-note beats (each the equivalent of three eighth notes). See also: *Simple time*.

Con *(45)* With.

Con brio, con fuoco, con spirito *(45)* Respectively, these terms mean 'with brilliance', 'with fire', 'with spirit'.

Concert pitch *(99)* The 'standard' pitches. Any instrument which isn't a transposing instrument – such as the piano, flute and violin – are said to play 'at concert pitch'. A 'concert pitch C' is a C played on any properly tuned non-transposing instrument. See also: *Transposing instruments*.

Consonant *(82–83)* Literally 'sounding together'. Consonant intervals are those which are traditionally thought of as pure and pleasant, not requiring resolution to other intervals. Consonant intervals can be subdivided into 'perfect' and 'imperfect' consonant intervals. See also: *Dissonant*.

Counting unit A term sometimes used to describe the bottom figure in a time signature. See also: *Time signature* and *Meter*.

Crescendo *(40)* Gradually get louder.

Crotchet The British term for quarter note. See: *Quarter note*.

Cut common time See: *Alla breve*.

Da Capo, D.C. *(59–60)* From the beginning. Often used in the instruction 'Da Capo al Fine': play from the beginning and finish at the marking 'Fine'.

Dal Segno, D.S. *(59)* From the sign. This marking tells the player to return to the 𝄋 sign and play from there.

Decrescendo *(40)* Gradually get quieter.

Degree See: *Step*.

Diatonic *(96)* The seven church modes, including what are now called major and minor, are the diatonic scales, each consisting of two half-tones and five whole tones. A passage of music can be described as diatonic if it sticks to these scales, using few or no accidentals. See also: *Church modes* and *Accidentals*.

Diminished *(79–81)* A diminished interval is a perfect interval which has been reduced by a half-tone. For example, C–G is a perfect fifth, so C–G♭ is a diminished fifth. Minor intervals reduced by a half-tone are also called diminished. See also: *Intervals* and *Perfect intervals*.

Diminuendo *(40)* Gradually get quieter.

Dissonant *(82–83)* Literally 'not sounding together'. Dissonant intervals are those which are traditionally considered to be harsh, and need to be 'resolved'. See also: *Consonant* and *Resolve*.

Do–Re–Mi *(14, 117)* The sequence of syllables Do–Re–Mi–Fa–So–La–Ti–Do are used as a way of teaching the major scale. In some countries, such as France, Do always represents C, and C major is indicated as 'Do Majeur'. However, in other countries Do is movable – so if you start Do–Re–Mi on an A♭, for example, you can sing the A♭ major scale.

Doit *(54–55)* A jazz ornament, involving a short upward bend of a note.

Dolce *(45)* Sweetly.

Dorian mode *(95)* The second church mode. See also: *Church modes*.

Dot, dotted *(23–25)* A dot after a note makes the note last one and a half times as long. A note with a dot is described as a 'dotted note'.

Double bar line *(57)* A bar line consisting of one thin line and one thick one. It is used at the end of pieces and combined with dots to make repeat signs.

Double flat *(38)* A note with a double flat sign (♭♭) is two half-tones lower than the natural note. See also: *Flat*.

Double sharp *(38)* A note with a double sharp sign (𝄪) is two half-tones higher than the natural note. See also: *Sharp*.

Downbeat *(104–105)* The first beat of a measure. See also: *Natural accents*.

Du-wah *(49–50)* An effect used mainly by jazz brass and wind players, involving the alternation of a muffled sound and an open sound.

Dur *(86)* The German term for major.

Dynamic markings *(39–41)* Signs and abbreviations – such as *p* and *ff* – that show how loudly or softly music should be played.

E flat instruments *(99)* Instruments that produce a concert pitch E♭ when the player reads and fingers a C. See also: *Transposing instruments.*

Eighth note *(7)* A note (♪) that lasts half the length of a quarter note.

Enharmonic *(32, 76, 80)* Any pair of notes, intervals or scales that sound the same, but have different names and look different on paper, are called enharmonic. For example, G♯ and A♭ are enharmonic notes, the augmented fourth and the diminished fifth are enharmonic intervals, and F sharp major (six sharps) and G flat major (six flats) are enharmonic scales.

Even eighths *(106)* See: *Straight eighths.*

F clef *(17)* Alternative name for the 'bass clef'. See: *Bass clef* and *Clef.*

Fall, fall off *(54–55)* A jazz ornament, which requires the player to 'fall' from the end of a note with a short downward glissando. See also: *Glissando.*

Fermata *(48)* A fermata, or pause, tells you to hold a note for as long as you like (or as long as the conductor or drummer wants you to).

Fifth *(74–75, 78, 81, 85)* An interval of five steps, such as from C to G (a 'perfect fifth'). See also: *Intervals.*

Fine *(59)* The end. See also: *Al Fine.*

Fingering Often on a piece of music, numbers appear above or below the notes. These suggest to the player which fingers to use to play the notes.

First-time ending *(58, 60)* When a section of music is repeated, the ending is often different the second time around. If this is the case, the first version is called the 'first-time' ending or measure, and the second version is called the 'second-time' ending or measure. The different endings are indicated with square brackets labelled 1 and 2.

Flat *(31–38, 67, 69–73)* 1. A symbol (♭) indicating that a note must be lowered by one half-tone. 2. Singing or playing that is out of tune because it's slightly too low is described as flat.

Flutter tonguing An effect used by wind players, who create a rapidly repeated note by rasping the tongue. See also: *Growling*.

Forte (*f*), **fortissimo** (*ff*), **fortississimo** (*fff*) *(39)* Respectively, these dynamic markings instruct you to play loudly, very loudly, and as loudly as possible.

Fortepiano (*fp*) *(41)* Loud, immediately followed by soft.

Four-four time *(11, 12)* A piece in four-four time or 'common time' has the time signature ⁴⁄₄ at the clef, or the symbol **C**. Every measure in such a piece lasts for four quarter-note beats. See also: *Time signature*.

Fourth *(77–78, 81, 84)* 1. An interval of four steps, such as from C to F (a 'perfect fourth'). 2. Quarter notes are occasionally referred to as 'fourth notes'.

See also: *Intervals*.

G clef *(17)* An alternative name for the 'treble clef'. See also: *Treble clef* and *Clef*.

Ghost note *(50)* A dead-sounding note, notated with a cross for a note head.

Glissando *(54)* A slide from one note to another.

Grace note *(53)* A type of ornament, consisting of a decorative note (written small with a line running through it) that precedes a normal note. Also called *acciaccatura*.

Grave Serious or earnest.

Growling A jazz technique. The player or singer creates a growling sound by using their tongue or throat, or by singing and playing simultaneously. See also: *Flutter tonguing*.

Gruppetto See: *Turn*.

Gypsy scale *(98)* A scale used in much East European folk music, which includes an interval of three half-tones in two places.

Half note *(6)* A type of note (♩), which lasts the same amount of time as two quarter notes.

Half-tone, half-step *(15, 64–66)* The smallest basic interval used in Western music; the distance between a note and its nearest neighbor, such as C–C♯ and E–F. However, in other cultures, and some modern Western music, even smaller intervals are used. Other names for the half-tone or half-step are 'semitone' and 'minor second'. See also: *Intervals* and *Tone*.

Harmonic minor *(88–90)* A version of the minor scale, usually used for harmony (chords). It has the seventh step raised by a half-tone. See also: *Minor scale*.

Hexatonic scale *(97)* See: *Whole-tone scale*.

Home note See: *Tonic*.

Imperfect consonance See: *Consonant*.

Interlude *(56)* 1. A piece that goes between and joins two other, larger pieces. 2. A section of a piece that acts as a bridge between two other sections.

Intervals *(77–85, 140–141)* An interval is the musical distance between one note and another. The basic intervals are named after the steps of a major scale: the second (such as C–D), the third (C–E), the fourth (C–F), and so on. Other intervals are described as altered versions of these with the terms 'augmented' (one half-tone larger), and 'diminished' or 'minor' (one half-tone smaller). Intervals can be subdivided into dissonant intervals, perfect consonant intervals and imperfect consonant intervals.

Inverted mordent *(51–52)* A one-note trill on the note below the written note.

Ionian mode *(86, 95)* The first church mode, which is the same as the major scale. See also: *Church modes* and *Major scale*.

Irregular meter, irregular time signature *(105)* A time signature in which the beats in each measure are subdivided into unequal groups. For example, a five-four measure can be subdivided into a group of three followed by a group of two (3+2), or vice versa (2+3). Such time signatures are also known as *odd meters* or *odd time signatures*. See also: *Time signature*.

Key *(34–35. 65–73. 91–94, 99)* The 'key' of music refers to the major or minor scale that it's based on. If a passage of music is 'in A major', then it will mainly contain notes of the A major scale (although other notes can also appear), and the note A will be the most important note – the 'tonic', or 'keynote'. If a whole piece is 'in A major', then it will usually start and end in A major, but may change to other keys ('modulate') in between. See also: *Scale*.

Keynote See: *Tonic*.

Key signature *(34–36, 69, 72, 90)* If a piece of music is written in any major or minor key, then the sharps or flats that appear in that key are written at the beginning of every stave, immediately after the clef. These sharps and flats (which apply throughout the piece) are the 'key signature'. See also: *Key*.

Largo, Larghetto *(43)* Largo is a very slow tempo (metronome marking 40–60). Larghetto is a little less slow (metronome marking 60–66). See also: *Metronome marking*.

Leading note, leading tone *(87–90)* The note one half-tone below the tonic of a key. This note naturally 'leads' to the tonic, and is also known as the 'subtonic'. See also: *Tonic*.

Ledger lines *(18)* Short extra lines drawn above and below the stave to extend its range.

Legato *(47)* Literally 'bound'. When a passage is played legato, each note flows smoothly to the next with no gap in between.

Lento Slow.

Lift *(55)* A type of ornament used in jazz, involving an upward glissando from a note. See also: *Glissando*.

Loco *(20)* Instruction to return to the written pitch, after a section marked *8va* or *8va bassa*. See also: *8va*.

Locrian mode *(95–96)* The seventh church mode. See also: *Church modes*.

Lydian mode *(95–96)* The fourth church mode. See also: *Church modes*.

Major scale *(63–70, 78–79, 86–87, 91, 142)* A type of scale consisting of tones and half-tones in the following order: T, T, H, T, T, T, H. Other names include the 'Ionian mode' and, in German, 'dur'.

Marcato *(48)* Literally 'marked'. A passage marked marcato should be played with little or no freedom of rhythm, with every note emphasized.

Measure *(10–12)* Music is divided into measures, or bars, by vertical lines (bar lines) drawn on the stave. Each contains a certain amount of time, divided into beats. See also: *Natural accents* and *Time signature*.

Medium, medium tempo *(43)* Tempo indication equivalent to a metronome marking of 100–120 BPM. See also: *Metronome marking*.

Melodic minor *(88–90)* The version of the minor scale used for melodies in classical music and some other styles. When it's going upwards, the sixth and seventh steps are raised by a half-tone; when it's going downward, it's the same as the straightforward natural minor. See also: *Minor scale*.

Meno *(45)* Literally 'less'. Used in combination with other instructions.

Meter *(29)* The way in which the beats of a piece are arranged into measures. Quadruple meter has

four beats per measure, triple meter has three, and duple meter has two. See also: *Time signature, Simple time* and *Compound time*.

Metronome *(42)* A mechanical or electronic device that ticks or beeps an adjustable steady beat. Used for practicing timing and rhythm skills.

Metronome marking *(42–43)* A metronome marking indicates how fast a piece should be played, expressed in terms of the number of beats per minute (BPM), which can be set on a metronome. The marking ♩ = 120, for example, means there should be 120 quarter notes every minute.

Mezzo-forte (*mf*) *(39)* Moderately loud.

Mezzo-piano (*mp*) *(39)* Moderately soft.

Middle C *(15, 18)* The C in the middle of the piano keyboard. This note is written one ledger line below the stave in the treble clef, and one ledger line above the stave in the bass clef.

Minim The British term for half note. See: *Half note*.

Minor scale *(63, 65–66,*

70–72, 86–90, 143) A scale consisting of tones and half-tones in the following order: T, H, T, T, H, T, T. Other names include the 'Aeolian mode' and, in German, 'moll'. In classical music and some other genres, various altered versions of the scale are used, including the 'harmonic minor' and the 'melodic minor'.

Mixolydian mode *(88, 95)* The fifth church mode. See: *Church modes.*

Modal music *(96)* Music based on of any church mode other than Ionian (major) and Aeolian (minor). See also: *Mode.*

Mode *(95–96)* This term can describe any system involving both a scale and a way of using the scale in Western or non-Western music. However, in Western music it usually refers specifically to the church modes. See also: *Church modes.*

Moderato *(43)* A medium tempo (metronome marking 108–120). See also: *Metronome marking.*

Modulate, modulation 1. *(72)* To move from one key to another. 2. *(52)* On keyboards and synthesizers, the modulation control simulates vibrato. See also: *Vibrato.*

Moll *(86–87)* The German term for minor. See also: *Minor scale.*

Molto *(45)* Literally 'much'.

Mordent *(51)* An ornament consisting of a one-note trill on the note above the written note.

Natural 1. *(34)* A sign (♮) which restores a note altered by a sharp (♯) or flat (♭) to its natural position. 2. *(15)* Any note played without a sharp or flat, such as 'A natural' or 'C natural'. On a keyboard instrument, these notes are the ones played on the white keys, so they are also sometimes referred to as the 'white notes'.

Natural accents *(104–105)* The accents that are 'built into' to a particular time signature. For example, in a four-four measure, beats 1 and to a lesser extent 3 are naturally accented. Other terms for such accents are 'strong beats', 'metric accents', 'accented beats', and 'on-beats'. The first beat of the measure is the 'downbeat', and the unaccented beats are the 'weak beats', or 'off-beats'.

Natural minor *(66)* The 'standard' minor scale (as found on the white keys of a keyboard from A to A) as opposed to the harmonic and melodic minor scales which have certain steps raised by a half-tone. See also: *Minor scale.*

Ninth *(81)* An interval of nine steps, such as from C to the D of the next octave (a major ninth), or from C to D♭ of the next octave (a minor ninth). See also: *Intervals.*

Non troppo *(45)* Literally 'not too much'.

Non-diatonic See: *Diatonic.*

Note *(5–10)* Either a single played sound, or a symbol representing one.

Note value *(9–10)* The amount of time that a note lasts for is its note value.

Octatonic scale *(97)* A scale made up of alternating half-tones and whole tones.

Octave *(14, 78, 80–91)* The interval of twelve half-tones which lies between two notes of the same name (such as one C and the next C). There's a system for naming specific octaves (see page 145).

Octavize *(20)* To play in a different octave. See also: *8va.*

Odd meter, odd time signature See: *Irregular meter.*

Original minor *(66)* See: *Natural minor.*

Ornamentation *(51–55)* In music, ornamentation is the decoration of a note or melody with embellishments such as short 'extra' notes and trills.

Outro *(56)* A section at the end of a song; the word often implies a fade-out. In jazz the term 'out chorus' is sometimes used to describe the final chorus of a tune in which all players improvise simultaneously.

Parallel keys *(91)* Two keys are 'parallel' if they have the same tonic, such as C major and C minor.

Part A piece of printed or written music that a player or players read from. A 'score' contains all the parts of a piece. In jazz, the term 'chart' is regularly used to mean either score or part.

Pentatonic scale *(98)* Any scale consisting of five different notes (*penta* = five). The most common type of pentatonic scale can be found by playing just the black notes on a keyboard instrument.

Perfect consonance See: *Perfect intervals.*

Perfect intervals *(78)* The perfect intervals are the most 'pure', 'consonant' intervals: the unison, the fourth, the fifth and the octave. See also: *Intervals.*

Phrase mark *(47)* A curved line indicating that a group of notes collectively form a single musical phrase, and so should be played as such.

Phrygian mode *(95)* The third church mode. See: *Church modes.*

Piano (*p*), **pianissimo** (*pp*), **pianississimo** (*ppp*) *(39)* Respectively, these dynamic markings instruct you to play quietly, very quietly, and as quietly as possible.

Pickup *(26)* See: *Upbeat.*

Pitch *(13–20)* The pitch of a note is how 'high' or 'low' it is.

Pitch bend *(45)* The 'bending' of the pitch of a note up or down.

Più *(45)* Literally 'more'.

Pizzicato, pizz. *(49)* On a bowed instrument, playing 'pizzicato' is plucking the strings with the fingers rather than playing them with the bow.

Plop *(55)* A short glissando down onto a note. The glissando usually comes before the beat, so the target note is on the beat.

Poco, poco a poco *(40, 44)* 'Poco' means 'a little bit' and 'poco a poco' means 'little by little'. The latter is often used in combination with the markings 'crescendo' (gradually get louder), and 'accelerando' (gradually get faster).

Postlude See: *Coda.*

Presto, prestissimo *(43)* Presto is a fast tempo (metronome marking 176–200), and prestissimo is a very fast tempo (metronome marking 200 or more). See also: *Metronome marking.*

Quarter note *(5)* A type of note (♩) which is usually counted as the beat.

Quaver The British term for eighth note. See: *Eighth note.*

Quintuplet *(28)* A group of five notes played in the space of one note (such as a quarter note, half note, etc).

Rallentando, rall. *(44)* Gradually get slower.

Range *(145)* The distance between the lowest and the highest notes that an instrument, player or singer can produce, usually expressed in octaves. A piano, for example, has a range of more than seven octaves.

Relative major, relative minor *(91)* Major and minor keys are 'relative' to each other if they share the same key signature. For example, F major and D minor each have one flat in their key signature; F major is the 'relative major' of D minor, and D minor is the 'relative minor' of F major.

Reminder accidental *(37)* A sharp, flat or natural symbol, often given in brackets, which is written to remind you that an accidental indicated earlier, or a sharp or flat in the key signature, still applies. See also: *Accidentals*.

Repeat signs *(57–59, 61–62)* Markings which indicate that a note, chord, measure or measures should be repeated.

Rest *(22–23)* A period of silence, or a symbol indicating one.

Resolve *(83)* A dissonant interval is 'resolved' when it is followed by the correct consonant interval. See also: *Dissonant* and *Consonant*.

Ritardando, ritard., rit. *(44)* Gradually get slower.

Ritenuto, riten., rit. *(44)* Gradually get slower. Some composers have used this term to imply a more sudden change of speed than 'ritardando' or 'rallentando', but usually there is no distinction.

Root, root-note The root of a chord is the note that it is based on and named after – such as the F in an F major triad. The term is sometimes also used to describe the 'tonic' or 'keynote', which is the note that a scale is based on.

Rubato *(43)* Play with freedom of tempo.

Scale *(63)* A series of notes arranged from low to high. In Western music, the term most commonly refers to the major and minor scales. See also: *Church modes, Major scale* and *Minor scale*.

Scoop *(49)* A jazz ornament entailing a slight bend of a note down and then back up.

Score A score is a printed or written piece of music which contains the parts of all instruments and singers in a piece. The term 'scoring' can be used to describe both the act of writing music down, and the act of arranging a work for different instruments.

Second *(78, 81, 84)* An interval of two steps, such as from C to D, or from C to D♭. See also: *Intervals*.

Second-time ending See: *First-time ending*.

Section lines See: *Bar lines*.

Section markings *(56–57)* Any symbols or words that mark the end and beginning of distinct sections.

Segno *(59)* The segno symbol (𝄋) marks a particular point in a piece of music. The instruction 'Dal Segno' tells you to return to that point. These markings are sometimes combined with other instructions, such as the coda sign.

Semibreve The British term for whole note. See *Whole note*.

Semiquaver The British term for sixteenth note. See: *Sixteenth note*.

Semitone See: *Half-tone*.

Septuplet *(28)* A group of seven notes played in the space of one note (such as a quarter note, half note, etc).

Seventh *(78, 81, 85)* An interval of seven steps such as from C to B, or C to B♭. See also: *Intervals*.

Sextuplet *(28)* A group of six notes played in the space of one note (such as a quarter note or half note, etc).

Sforzando, sf, sfz *(41)* Play with extra force. Although it looks like a dynamic marking, sforzando is really a kind of accent – it only refers to the note or chord that it's written under.

Sharp *(31–38, 67, 69–73)* 1. The symbol (♯) indicating that a note must be raised by one half-tone. 2. Singing or playing that is out of tune because it's slightly too high is described as sharp.

Simile *(48)* Keep playing the same way. If this marking is written, for example, after a few staccato notes, you should keep playing staccato until you're instructed to stop.

Simple time, simple meter *(29)* Any time signature, such as four-four and two-two, where the beat is not a dotted note. See also: *Meter* and *Compound time*.

Sixteenth note *(7)* A type of note (♬) which lasts for a quarter of the time of one quarter note.

Sixth *(78, 81, 85)* An interval of six steps, such as from C to A (a major sixth), or from C to A♭ (a minor sixth). See also: *Intervals*.

Slur *(47)* A curved line binding two notes of different pitches, implying they should be played 'legato' – smoothly with no gap between them. A 'tie' looks the same but connects notes of the same pitch, and turns them into a single note. See also: *Tie*.

Solfège *(83)* Another term for 'aural training' or 'ear training', which involves practicing your ability to recognize melodies, chords and rhythm 'by ear'.

Staccato, staccatissimo *(46–47)* Staccato, indicated by a dot below or above a note, instructs you to play the note slightly short and clipped. Staccatissimo, indicated with a small triangle under or above the note, tells you to play the note very short and clipped.

Staff Another name for stave. See: *Stave*.

Stave *(16–18)* The five horizontal lines used for the notation of music. Also referred to as *staff*.

Step *(64)* 1. A certain note in a scale or mode – the second step of a scale is the second note of the scale. Also known as 'degree'. 2. Sometimes, the term step is used to mean a whole tone (such as C–D), and 'half-step' is used to mean a half-tone (such as C–D♭). See also: *Tone* and *Half-tone*.

Straight eighths *(106)* A term implying that the eighth notes in a piece should be played as exact eighth notes, rather than with 'swing' (with a 'triplet feel'). The term 'even eighths' means the same thing. See also: *Swing*.

Stringendo, string. *(44)* Gradually get faster.

Swing *(106)* If the word swing is written at the beginning of a piece of music, it tells you to read the eighth notes with a 'triplet feel' – as if each group of two eighth notes were the first and last notes in a eighth-note triplet. What swing means in general is difficult to define, but it can relate to any playing which is subtly 'against' the beat. See also: *Straight eighths*.

Tablature, tab *(109–110)* Any system of writing down music other than staves and notes. The most common example is guitar tablature.

Tempo *(42–45)* The tempo of music is the speed at which it is played.

Tempo markings *(42–45)* Indications of how fast a piece should be played, usually expressed in Italian or English words, or metronome markings. See also: *Metronome marking*.

Tempo I°, tempo primo See: *A tempo*.

Tenuto *(48)* An accent where you 'lean' on a note, making it slightly longer and perhaps a little louder. Also called 'agogic accent'.

Tetrachord *(96)* Any diatonic scale consists of two halves, called tetrachords. C major, for example, consists of the tetrachords C–D–E–F and G–A–B–C.

Third *(77, 81, 84)* An interval of three steps, such as from C to E (a major third), or from C to E♭ (a minor third). See also: *Intervals*.

Three-four *(11–12)* A piece with a time signature of three-four ($\frac{3}{4}$) has three quarter-note beats in each measure. See also: *Time signatures*.

Tie *(25)* A curved line connecting two notes of the same pitch to make one longer note. When two notes are 'tied', the second one is not played separately but simply held on. See also: *Slur*.

Time signature *(11–12, 104–105)* A time signature indicates how many beats there are in each measure and what type of note the beat is.

In pieces with a four-four time signature ($\frac{4}{4}$) every measure has four beats, and each beat is one quarter note long. The time signature is written at the beginning of a piece (and elsewhere if it changes).

Tone 1. *(15)* Another term for a 'whole tone' (or 'whole step', or 'major second'), which is an interval of two half-tones, such as C–D, or A♭–B♭. 2. The specific sound made by an instrument or player. 3. Occasionally, the word tone is used instead of the word note.

Tonic *(63)* The tonic is the note which a scale is based on and named after, such as C in C major. Other terms are 'keynote', 'home note' and (incorrectly) 'root'.

Tranquillo *(45)* Calmly.

Transition *(56)* A mainly classical term for a part of a piece which moves from one section to another, usually changing key in the process.

Transpose, transposition *(99–103)* To transpose is to take a piece of music and play or write it in another key.

Transposing instruments *(99–101)* Transposing instruments produce different notes from those that the player reads and fingers. When an alto saxophonist, for example, reads and fingers a C, the resulting note is actually an E♭. So the alto sax is said to be 'in E flat' or an 'E flat instrument'.

Treble clef *(17)* A clef that sets the second line of the stave as the G above middle C. It's also called the 'G clef'. See also: *Clef*.

Tremolo *(52–53)* A quick repetition of one note, or a rapid alternation between two notes.

Trill *(51)* A rapid alternation between two adjacent notes.

Triplet *(26–28)* Three notes played in space of one (a quarter note, half note, etc). Triplets are indicated by a number 3 written above or below the notes, often with a square or curved bracket.

Triplet feel *(106)* See: *Swing*.

Tritone *(81)* Another name for the interval of an augmented fourth, such as C–F♯. The term comes from the fact that such an interval consists of three whole tones (C–D, D–E, E–F♯). See also: *Intervals*.

Turn *(54)* An ornament involving the playing of a specific pattern of decorative notes. Also called *gruppetto*.

Unison Literally 'one sound'.

1. *(77)* The name given to the 'non-interval' between two notes of the same pitch. 2. If two musicians are playing the same line they are said to be playing 'in unison'. See also: *Intervals*.

Upbeat 1. *(26)* A note or a few notes in an incomplete measure at the beginning of a piece, which form a lead-in to the first beat of the first full measure. Also called a 'pickup' and, in classical music, an 'anacrusis'. 2. (105) The last beat in a measure. The term comes from the fact that a conductor usually signals this beat by moving the baton or hand in an upwards motion.

Vibrato *(52–53)* A note played or sung with vibrato oscillates slightly up and down in pitch.

Vivace *(45)* Lively.

Weak beats See: *Natural accents*.

White notes, white keys 1. The white keys on a keyboard instrument. 2. A general term for the natural notes. See also: *Natural*.

Whole note *(6)* A type of note (o) which lasts the same amount of time as four quarter notes.

Whole tone *(15)* Also called 'tone'. An interval of two half-tones (such as C–D). Not to be confused with the *whole note*, which is a note that lasts as long as four quarter notes. See also: *Intervals*.

Whole-tone scale *(97)* A scale made up entirely of whole-tone steps. Whole-tone scales are also called 'hexatonic scales', as each consists of six different notes. See also: *Intervals*.

WANT TO KNOW MORE?

This book gives you the information you need in order to read music, and provides you with the basics of music theory. If you're keen to know more, there are hundreds of books and Web sites you could consult.

A book about harmony (chords) would make an ideal follow up to this book. Many books deal specifically with classical harmony, but some, such as the popular *Harmony & Theory: A Comprehensive Source for All Musicians* by Keith Wyatt and Carl Schroeder (Musicians Institute Press), are more general. There are quite a few books on jazz theory and harmony – *The Jazz Theory Book* by Mark Levine (Sher Music Co) is considered by many as the best. When it comes to other styles, books tend to deal with a particular instrument and genre, such as blues piano or rock guitar.

Exercises
Lots of ear-training methods are available (many of which come with a tape or CD), as well as whole books of scales, sight-reading and other exercises for each instrument.

The Internet
The Internet contains lots of information about music theory. Some sites, such as www.musictheory.net and www.musictheory.halifax.ns.ca, have courses, quizzes and even an email query service. Searching for 'music theory' usually brings up quite a few relevant pages, though if you have a particular problem, you'll generally have more success searching for something more specific.

ESSENTIAL REFERENCE

In this chapter you'll find various things which are good to have at hand for immediate reference. It includes the major and minor scales written out on staves, a do-it-yourself scale wheel, the circle of fifths, some memory aids, and the systems of naming specific notes and octaves.

When photocopied and assembled, the scale wheel on the opposite page shows you which notes are in each major and minor scale, and tells you the names of the intervals within an octave.

Assembly
Photocopy the two circles, cut them out, glue them onto card, and fix them together with a cotter pin. The outer part is a one-octave keyboard, made into a circle.

Scales
If you want to find out the notes of a major scale, point 'TONIC MAJOR' at the tonic note of the scale. The black arrows will point to the notes of the scale. For the minor scales use 'TONIC MINOR'.

Intervals
In order to find the name of an interval between two notes, point the 'TONIC MAJOR' at the lower note, and read the name of the interval from the arrow which is pointing at the upper note. Maj. stands for major; min. stands for minor; aug. stands for augmented; dim. stands for diminished.

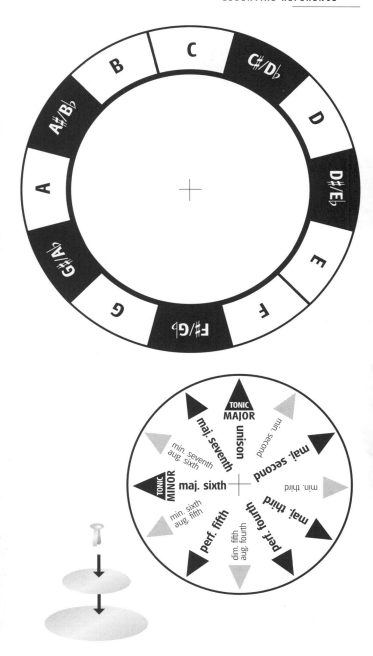

Photocopy this page, cut the circles out, and cotter-pin them together through the centres

141

THE MAJOR AND MINOR SCALES

The major and minor scales are the two most commonly used scales in Western music. Here are the most important ones written out on staves. Chapters 11 and 14 deal with the theory of major and minor.

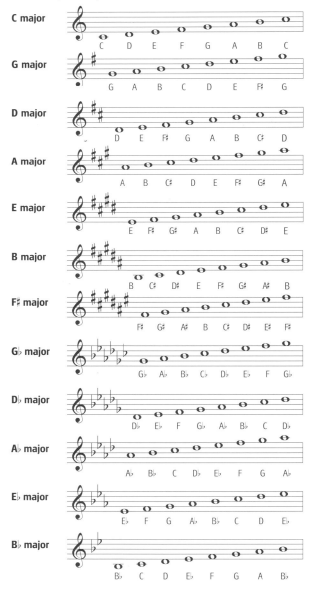

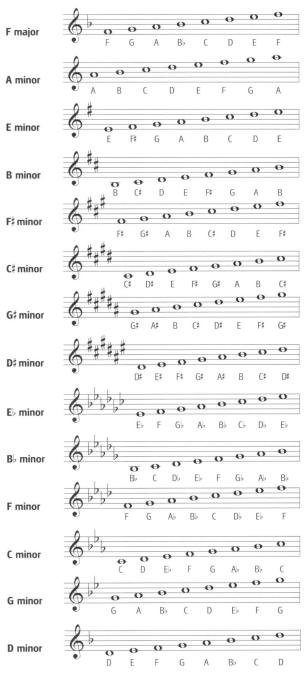

F major
F G A B♭ C D E F

A minor
A B C D E F G A

E minor
E F♯ G A B C D E

B minor
B C♯ D E F♯ G A B

F♯ minor
F♯ G♯ A B C♯ D E F♯

C♯ minor
C♯ D♯ E F♯ G♯ A B C♯

G♯ minor
G♯ A♯ B C♯ D♯ E F♯ G♯

D♯ minor
D♯ E♯ F♯ G♯ A♯ B C♯ D♯

E♭ minor
E♭ F G♭ A♭ B♭ C♭ D♭ E♭

B♭ minor
B♭ C D♭ E♭ F G♭ A♭ B♭

F minor
F G A♭ B♭ C D♭ E♭ F

C minor
C D E♭ F G A♭ B♭ C

G minor
G A B♭ C D E♭ F G

D minor
D E F G A B♭ C D

THE CIRCLE OF FIFTHS

You can read all about the circle of fifths in Chapters 12 and 14.

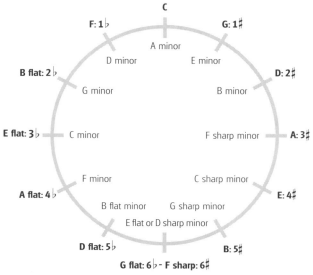

KEY SIGNATURES

The order of sharps and flats in key signatures is fully discussed in Chapters 5, 11 and 12. Here's a memory aid to help you learn the order by heart. Remember that the sentence for flats is exactly the reverse of the sentence for sharps.

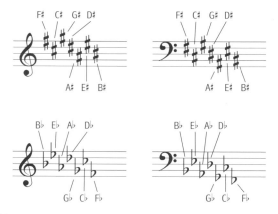

Order of the sharps: F♯, C♯, G♯, D♯, A♯, E♯, B♯.
(Father Charles Goes Down And Ends Battle).

Order of the flats: B♭, E♭, A♭, D♭, G♭, C♭, F♭.
(Battle Ends And Down Goes Charles' Father).

OCTAVES AND NOTE NAMES

There are a variety of systems used to name the various octaves and the notes within them. Confusingly, the different systems contradict each other, so you need to know what system is being used before you know which note is being referred to. The table below shows the names of the octaves: the contra octave is the one from the lowest C upwards on the piano keyboard and the one-line octave goes upwards from middle C. The notes in the octaves are named as shown in the table – the most common systems are shown in the first two columns. As you can see, middle C can be written as c', C4 or c, depending on the system used.

Name of octave	Common systems		Other systems	
contra octave	C₁–B₁	C1–B1	CCC–BBB	C2–B2
great octave	C–B	C2–B2	CC–BB	C1–B1
small octave	c–b	C3–B3	C–B	C–B
one-line octave	c'–b'	C4–B4	c–b	c–b
two-line octave	c''–b''	C5–B5	c'–b'	c1–b1
three-line octave	c'''–b'''	C6–B6	c''–b''	c2–b2
four-line octave	c''''–b''''	C7–B7	c'''–b'''	c3–b3
five-line octave	c'''''–b'''''	C8–B8	c''''–b''''	c4–b4

Ranges

These systems are often used to describe an instrument or singer's range. In the terms of the common systems, for instance, the classical guitar has a range of E–b'', or E2–B5.

Even lower

The lowest octave shown in the table starts on the lowest C on the piano, but there are even lower notes. The next octave down is known as the *sub-contra octave*, usually written as C₁₁–B₁₁ or C0–B0.

MUSIC ROUGH GUIDES ON CD

'Like the useful Rough Guide travel books and television shows, these discs delve right into the heart and soul of the region they explore'
— *Rhythm Music (USA)*

Available from book and record shops worldwide or order direct from World Music Network, Unit 6, 88 Clapham Park Road, London SW4 7BX tel: 020 7498 5252 • fax: 020 7498 5353 • email: post@worldmusic.net

Hear samples from over 50 Rough Guide CDs at
WWW.WORLDMUSIC.NET

Will you have enough stories to tell your grandchildren?

©2001 Yahoo! Inc.

Yahoo! Travel

Do You YAHOO!?

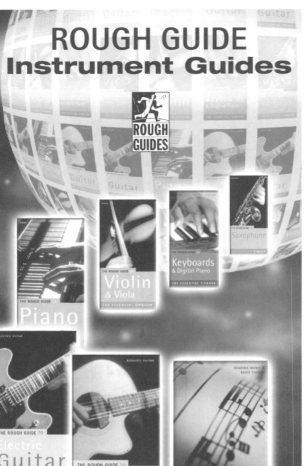

ROUGH GUIDE
Instrument Guides

ROUGH GUIDES

Keyboards & Digital Piano

Violin & Viola

Saxophone

Piano

Electric Guitar & Bass Guitar

Acoustic Guitar

Reading Music & Basic Theory

ESSENTIAL TIPBOOK
SERIES

August 2001

Clarinet

Flute